Shakara Bridgers,
Jeniece Isley, and
Joan A. Davis

Recipe Consultant
Therese Nelson

The
Get 'Em Girls'
Guide to
the Perfect
Get-Together

A Fireside Book

Published by Simon & Schuster

New York   London   Toronto   Sydney

Fireside
A Division of Simon & Schuster, Inc.
1230 Avenue of the Americas
New York, NY 10020

First Fireside trade paperback edition May 2009

FIRESIDE and colophon are registered trademarks of Simon & Schuster, Inc.

For information about special discounts for bulk purchases,
please contact Simon & Schuster Special Sales at
1-800-456-6798 or business@simonandschuster.com

Designed by Kerry DeBruce, Ruth Lee-Mui
Photos by Piper Carter
Cover art by Jenn Crute

Manufactured in the United States of America

1 3 5 7 9 10 8 6 4 2

Library of Congress Cataloging-in-Publication Data
Bridgers, Shakara.
The get 'em girls' guide to the perfect get-together / Shakara Bridgers,
Jeniece Isley, and Joan A. Davis. — 1st Fireside trade paperback ed.
p.   cm.
"A Fireside Book."
1. Entertaining.   2. Cookery, American.   3. Menus.
I. Isley, Jeniece.   II. Davis, Joan A.   III. Title.
TX731.B72   2009
793.2 — dc22   2008028596

ISBN-13: 978-1-4165-8777-4
ISBN-10:   1-4165-8777-2

This book is dedicated to our mothers,
"The Original Get 'Em Girls"

Contents

Acknowledgments

Jeniece

Once again, I want to say thank you, Lord, for continuing to bless me and this journey. Every time I think I've reached the finish line, you bless me some more . . . that's love!

Mommy, you're the best! Thank you for your continuous support — I got lucky when I got you. Daddy, I'm still not taking any wooden nickels; thank you for watching out for me! I love and miss you. Crystal, as long as I owe you, you'll never be broke . . . and I owe you a whole lot! Thanks for being the best big sister in the world! Kayla, you've grown so much. You're a teenager now (ill), but you will always be my baby — I love you. DTC, from BBW parties to this . . . 10 years and counting, baby, and I'm loving every minute of it. I hope you know how proud I am of you! Thank you for all the love and support that you give.

Shakara, in the words of Patti LaBelle, "If you only knew, how much I do, do love you!" I can't even find the words to say how blessed I am to call you my friend and my business partner. Joan, thank you for understanding my craziness. As the voice of reason and the referee, you see what it's really like to be my friend . . . thanks for putting up with me, I love you. E-Dub, we'se family now (*sic*)! You are a direct reflection of how good God is: 12-hour days, attitudes, deadlines, and no pay . . . who does that? Therese, you are a blessing, thank you for everything. Amithy, thank you for being my "Gayle." Shanya and Justin, I love you two crazy kids; stay beautiful and sweet. Nazae, I'm a deadbeat godmommy, but I love you still. Danielle, thank you for the years of friendship.

To my extended family and friends, thank you for the love and support! To every last one of my family members: Isley, Washington, Neal, Lowe, McDonald, and on and on . . . I love you! Mrs. Sandra K and Hilton, I know it's expensive to believe in us, but you do it anyway. I love you! Dwayne, Kirsten and Blaze, Bertina and Charlay, Dorian, Khalil, Badu, Leah, Valerie, Russ, and Cheryl, thank you for your support, your ear, your welcome arms, your love . . . I love you!

Shakara

God—you are my refuge. Every day we get closer. You've never failed me. Continue to make me over.

Mommy—you are a warrior, a survivor! What did I ever do to deserve you as a parent? I love you, thanks for always supporting me. Where would the Get 'Em Girls be without you and your credit card? Daddy—I am happy to be your daughter. Thanks for teaching me how to be "cool." Tanitsha—I'm so proud of you, lil' sis! Grandma—I love you so much. Thanks for always listening and believing in my dreams.

Hilton—you are the best bartender and stepfather I know. Thanks for always coming through to bail me out.

Aunt Joyce, Aunt Renee, Aunt Andrea, Aunt Sharon, Uncle James, Uncle Michael, and Uncle Ricky—I love all of you. Thanks for your support throughout the years. Damon—an empire will await you. Leonard—keep pushing, Rome wasn't built in a day. Andrenique—you have grown into a beautiful teenager. Call me if you need me. Cochise—I understand you more than you know . . . love ya!

Jamal aka Jagged Edge—I will outdo you, just wait! CJ, La John, Tory, Steven, and Shannon—we are all cut from the same cloth; entrepreneurship is in our blood. Stay focused! Mia, Ryan, Cathy, Michelle, Ursula, Emika—thanks for supporting your crazy cousin. To the Bridgers, Browns, Fonvilles, Sherrods, and Mills—I am proud to have you as family. Aunt Freat—thanks for the recipes!

Resonda, Tori, Tasha, Crystal—what would I do without you all? You all are great best friends and mothers. You all inspire me. I work hard for us.

LB, Nakia Janee, Morgan, Yalaina, Briana, Rasheed, Rashad, Sydney, Sierra, Kayla, Curtis, Curtis, Corey—you all are growing like weeds! Enjoy your youth.

Moms aka "the O.G. Get 'Em Girl"—thanks for always feeding and believing in me.

Jeniece—my sister from another mother. Girl, we made it. I wouldn't mind being homeless as long as you were next to me.

Joan—I am immune to the lashes . . . lol . . . thanks for keeping the bank account, Jeniece, and me balanced. Love ya!

Dee (Big Brotha) and Dwayne—thanks for the laughs. Beyoncé is no Gwen Guthrie . . . lol. Love ya'll.

Eric—I always said I wanted a younger brother and 32 years later God gave me you. Thanks for believing in Get 'Em Girl, Inc., before the check. Your seat at *Oprah* is reserved. Kool-Aid for everyone!

Dr. Sean P. Gardner—thanks for welcoming me into Eastward Baptist Church. I don't know how your number ended up in my speed dial, but forgive me for all the late nights I didn't put my phone on lock and called you by mistake.

Chef Therese—your passion for food excites me. You are the "Essential Seasoning" for Get 'Em Girls Catering!

Vonetta—I'm here now, love ya.

Kyle T.—Flight 817 changed my life. Thanks for being a great friend and spades partner. Love you, Sunshine!

Friends make the world go round—Connell, Peter, Leah, Valerie, Jango, CL, Troy Marshall, Gary, Brandi, Lavel, Jeremy, Kyjuan, Ash, Don, Amithy, Damian, Shawn Holiday, Phoenix, Will Gordon (hug), Dirty, Kirsten, Shani Kulture, Beasley (remind me to never invite you to Boot Camp class again), Kasey the Great, Autumn, Ellen, Marcus and Natasha Kelly, Johnny "NuBuzz" Nunez, Veronica, JB, Kenny, Khalil, Hassan (Bartendaz!), Olympia, Kerry, Bre, Courie aka "Hollywood," and the Kinston High School Class of 94.

Thanks to Jennifer Crute, Nadine, Sherise, Terrell, Piper Carter, and Dani for all of your support. You worked for Get 'Em Girls, Inc., when a check was only a dream.

To the love of my life, "Hip Hop"—thanks for inspiring me to believe and invest in me.

Joan

God, thank you once again for bringing my vision to fruition, thanks for your guidance and discernment!

Mommy, you are wonderful; thanks for always being loving, giving, caring, and prayerful. To my family, thank you for your love and support; your enthusiasm keeps me motivated.

Rev. Dr. J.G. McCann, Sr., and everyone at St. Luke Baptist Church—your outpour of love and support will forever be cherished; you guys really know how to make a girl feel special!

To my friends and extended family—thank you, thank you, thank you—I love you guys and you're stuck with me forever! Ms. Cookie—thanks for always being there when we need you. Eric Nunlee, I am so grateful for everything you've done for us; you're a major asset to our team. Therese, you complete our team; thanks for all that you do. Margo, thank you for believing! To everyone in the Low country, thank you so much for supporting me! Keya Neal, Henry Smalls, and everyone at It's All in the Cut Salon—thank you!

Jeniece and Shakara, so far this has been one deliciously enchanted journey and I'm enjoying every minute of it . . . let's go Get 'Em!

The Get 'Em Girls would like to thank Nadine, Sherise, Sulay, Shawna, and the Simon & Schuster staff. CL, Will, Neil, and the Digiwaxx Staff, Lisa, Asiana, Ladies of WEEN, Syreta, Felicia, Tamika and Dawn (Trax Hair Salon), Piper Carter, Terell Belin, Jenn Crute, Johnny Nunez, Kerry DeBruce, Nova, Brandi, Kristian, and Byron.

Introduction

Get-Together: An assembly or informal gathering of family and friends.

So you met the man of your dreams and the two of you have been cooking, eating, and spending every free moment together; after months of being missing in action from your friends, you finally decide to come up for air (which is great because your girlfriends were moments away from setting up an intervention). The *Get 'Em Girls' Guides* are about investing time in your relationships; not just with your new man, but with your family and friends as well. Did you really think it was all about getting and keeping a man? You've got to have a balance to keep your man *and* your friends. There is no better way to reacquaint yourself with family and friends than with a perfect get-together. Besides, how else do you expect to find out what's been going on since you were last seen out in public?

We're assuming you've purchased *The Get 'Em Girls' Guide to the Power of Cuisine*, so we know you have all your staples in your pantry, and cooking equipment, you know how to set a table properly, and can pick the right wines to complement your meal. Now let's move on to entertaining! Entertaining can be a little intimidating, but don't worry—we made sure to give you a few basic elements that will help your soiree go over without a hitch. Here is one lesson we learned that definitely comes in handy when having a fabulous get-together: Proper planning prevents a poor party (yes, we know that's not exactly the way the old adage goes, but we remixed it).

We have compiled a list of everything a person would need to host a great event, from tips on setting the mood, wine 102, 8 reasons to host a get-together, and of course *fabtastic* (that's fabulous and fantastic) menu selections for bridal and baby showers, fight parties, Sweet Sixteen soirees, meet-the-family brunch, or a simple light bite with the girls. Whether you're inspired to host a get-together because of a new home, new love, new baby, new flat-screen TV, or just because — your guests will be left talking about your wonderful event long after the music stops playing and the wine has stopped pouring.

8 Reasons to Host a Get-Together

1 What's better than getting together with friends and family? Any time spent in the presence of your loved ones is a beautiful time—and well worth the effort of fixing a fabulous meal prepared with love.

2 Party more and stress less. Hosting small, casual parties is easier and way less stressful. You'll find that you actually have time to enjoy the party with your guests.

3 First impressions are everything! And you want to make the best impression possible when meeting your sweetie's family and friends.

4 You are the life of the party. Anyone who has ever invited you to a backyard barbecue or a party that they've hosted knows all too well that the party doesn't start until you walk through the door—now it's *your* turn to get the party started!

5 Eating out with friends can get expensive—and there are better ways to spend your money, like at a fabulous shoe sale! Most get-togethers are inexpensive to put together, since there is no need for formal table settings, the decorations are minimal, and the meal is casual—which leaves just enough change left over for that secret sample sale you just got an invite to!

6 People will appreciate your effort and hospitality. Between the delectable food and great conversations, your friends will be eagerly anticipating the next get-together.

7 **You deserve to shine.** We have said it before, and we are saying it again: It's perfectly okay to toot your own horn. You've worked hard perfecting your culinary skills and now you are a B. Smith in the making—relish it!

8 **Last but not least—you are a Get 'Em Girl!** Once again, no explanation needed!

Plan of Action

*b*efore you do anything, create a plan. Even for a small get-together, having a plan will help immensely with everything from going to the market for groceries to putting together the invite list.

If this is the first gathering you've hosted, you probably feel like a fish out of water. We all can't be Martha, but you do know what *you* like when you go to get-togethers. Whether it was the beautiful tray of fresh fruits accompanied by white chocolate fondue that was set out for everyone to enjoy or something as simple as the name tags on each chair at your best friend's dinner party—whatever it is that you enjoyed about the last party you attended, try to incorporate those elements into your get-together in a unique and personalized way. So take a moment and a couple of deep breaths and relax.

Decide on a theme.

Before you send out the first invite, figure out why it is you want to host a get-together. Once you get that out of the way, work on a theme—whether it is a birthday celebration or a just-because cocktail party, you want to create a menu and an invite list that will make this a gathering that is comfortable and fun for everyone.

Make a to-do list.

Writing down everything you need *before* going shopping for your get-together makes for a more effective and less expensive trip. You don't know how many times one of us has gone shopping for something that we needed for an event . . . and managed to pick up everything but what we set out to get; and before you know it, we've spent fifty bucks on margarita glasses and forgotten to pick up the tequila. Take inventory of all the serving utensils, glasses, plates, etc., that you have to make sure you won't run out in the middle of your get-together.

Know your guests.

This *should* be the easiest part of planning a get-together, but you would be surprised how many times we've made the mistake of inviting two people who have been having issues to a small gathering—it doesn't always make for good company. Now, I know you are probably like, "that isn't my problem," but unless you enjoy playing referee, try your best to create a drama-free environment. If all else fails, call the individuals prior to your event, forewarning them of each other's attendance—one of them might back out, and your drama problem will be solved!

Try store-bought shortcuts.

You will make your life much easier by taking advantage of some store-bought items. Fruit and cheese trays are readily available in many larger supermarkets— take advantage of them. Large bowls of multicolored tortillas served with salsa are great for predinner snacking.

Portion control.

When shopping and preparing dishes for your get-together, specifically where finger foods are being served, plan for at least two portions per guest, before the meal. If you're just serving finger foods, we suggest you double that!

When it comes to drinks, plan for at least three drinks per person. Make sure to include nonalcoholic drink options as well.

Preparing for a wide array of menu options makes for happy guests. As a guide, assume that a couple of your friends have converted to vegetarianism and make two or three vegetarian dishes. A couple of people may be watching their diets, so prepare some healthful options, and so on.

To B.(Y.O.B.) or not?

Okay, this is a tricky one. Ideally, we'd say you provide the food and the drinks, but if you're hosting an informal get-together, why not have your guests bring the wine, beer, or spirits? Now, if the get-together is less "Fight Night Bash" and more "Meet the Parents Dinner Party," we suggest you dust off a bottle or two of red and white from your wine rack and play the attentive hostess that we know you are.

Set the Mood

*g*reat get-togethers live in your guests' memories long after the last alcohol and hors d'oeuvres have been devoured. The demand to plan the perfect get-together may be overwhelming; however, if you pace yourself and follow your plan of action, your get-together is sure to be a success.

Invitations

As with any party, the invitation that you send will set the stage for the upcoming event. Whether by mail, hand, or e-vite, invitations reveal so much about your event—the mood, the tone, the atmosphere. So choose one that will really spark interest and excitement among your guests. Your invitation should scream "This is the party of the year," not "I'll attend if no reruns of *Martin* are on." Be clear about time, location, attire, activities, and anything else that may be involved in your get-together.

Candles

Candles are a great way to set the mood of your event with colors or scents of flowers and foods. Candles can create a calm and peaceful environment for your affair. Whether you are having a day or evening get-together, candles add an ambience no other piece of décor can. Candles are inexpensive, eye-catching, and will bring your get-together to life.

Music

Whether you've hired a DJ or you have the mp3 player mix to die for, music is always a welcome addition to any get-together. Choosing the appropriate music for your get-together is critical. Your music selections should be as easy to digest as the food you have prepared. Depending on the event, you might want to keep the background music in the background, allowing your guests to enjoy conversing.

Dinner and barware

Sometimes there is nothing wrong with being a Plain Jane. When selecting dinnerware, you can't go wrong with white. White dinnerware is versatile and allows you the freedom to be creative when setting your tablescape. Your food will pop on white dinnerware and you can accent it with various centerpieces and table linens. The same goes for selecting your barware. When in doubt, stick with clear glasses. Clear glasses will easily match your dinnerware and also highlight the colors of your delicious drinks.

Wine 102

We know that planning an entertaining menu and a fabulous evening for guests can sometimes feel like a daunting experience, but don't worry; with proper planning and our helpful tips, you're guaranteed to have a good time at your own party. Just think about it—some of the fondest memories have been made sitting around the dinner table with family and friends, laughing, feeling scrumptiously full and somewhat tipsy.

How much wine do I purchase?

To begin, we know one of the first questions people tend to ask when hosting an event is: How much wine should I get? A 750ml wine bottle yields five to six servings per bottle, and you figure each guest will consume one glass every hour; so simply multiply the number of people times the length of your party in hours and you've got a good idea of how much wine you should purchase.

What kind of wine to buy?

The type of wine to purchase will depend on what type of event you're hosting. For white wine, consider having two options. A good Chardonnay will pair well with many different menus, and for a second white wine option, consider having a Sauvignon Blanc or Pinot Grigio. Having two really good red wines is just as important—serve a Cabernet Sauvignon and a Merlot and your guests will be completely satisfied.

Serving temperatures

The temperature at which you serve your wine greatly affects the wine's taste. When wine is served too cold or too warm, it can lose its delightful characteristics. There is an old rumor that red wines should be served at room temperature and white wines should be served right out of the fridge, but the average room is 70°F, which is way too warm to serve anything except coffee, and the average refrigerator temperature is 35°F, which is good for lettuce—not wine.

Once again, the Get 'Em Girls have you covered. Below is a simple primer with serving temperatures to help you out.

Type of Wine	Temperature	Serving Temperature
Chardonnay, Pinot Grigio, and Riesling	Slightly chilled	50–55°F
Sauvignon Blanc, Sparkling, and Dessert Wine	Chilled	42–45°F
Champagne	Chilled	40–43°F
Merlot, Bordeaux, Shiraz, and Cabernet Sauvignon	Cellar temperature	57–62°F

Go, Shorty, It's Your Birthday

All About the Kids
Chicken Fingers
Pigs in a Blanket
Grilled PB&J Cut-Out Sandwiches
Veggie Bites with Buttermilk Ranch Dip
Shakara's Fruit Punch
DIY (Decorate It Yourself) Yellow Cupcakes with Easy Buttercream Frosting

Sweet Sixteen Soiree
Sausage and Pepperoni Pizza Tarts
Macaroni and Cheese Bites
Chocolate Bonbons
Get 'Em Girl Shimosas (page 206)

Whether your precious baby just turned 6 or 16, one of the many joys (and pains) of parenthood is throwing a fabulous birthday party. We are sure you've seen those infamous Sweet Sixteen episodes that have you looking at the television like "Who in the heck . . ." and left your child anxiously awaiting their sixteenth birthday soiree. At this point, you need to sit your baby on down and express to them that although their birthday party will be fabulous, you will not be taking out a second mortgage on the house to have baby tigers walk them out to greet their friends. However, being the Get 'Em Girl that you are, not only will the party still be fabulous, the food will be absolutely delicious!

Here are some tips for planning a successful party for a child of any age:

Keep the food familiar, simple, and delicious.

Today is not the day to try and introduce a group of hungry children to the new prune and pomegranate cobbler you've been working on for the last 30 days.

Have fun activities planned.

You can plan a simple dance contest for the Chris Brownesque teens, or set up a create-your-own tee shirt table, overflowing with fabric paints, rhinestones, and stencils.

Keep the music clean and current.

We know you want to break out your *Marvin Gaye's Greatest Hits* CD, but remember this party is for the kids. Sit down with your child and create a playlist tailored to both of your likings; and if a DJ is not in the budget, a digital media player plugged into the speakers will work perfectly fine.

Have a theme.

An '80s themed party would be cool—complete with '80s candies, graffiti backdrops, and a break-dancing contest. A great parting gift for each guest would be a tee shirt with their name spray painted on the back . . . in pure '80s style, of course.

Fun food ideas.

Ice cream sundae bar, chocolate fountains, vases filled with M&M's in the party's colors on each table, and instead of traditional birthday cake, roll out a cupcake tree and let each child decorate their own cupcake with whatever they like—from sprinkles to chocolate morsels!

Get 'Em Girl Essential Seasoning

2 tablespoons kosher salt

2 teaspoons sugar

1 teaspoon paprika

½ teaspoon turmeric

¼ teaspoon onion powder

¼ teaspoon garlic powder

We use this spice blend on everything from eggs to our favorite sauces. It's great on just about anything. Enjoy!

Combine all ingredients in a small bowl and mix well. Will store for up to six months in a jar with a tight-fitting lid.

Makes about ¼ cup

Chicken Fingers

*t*hese are absolutely a must-have for any child's party. What child doesn't love chicken fingers?

1 Cut each chicken breast lengthwise into four strips and season with the Seasoning. Place the flour, eggs, and corn flake crumbs into three separate shallow bowls. Season the flour with salt and pepper. Dredge the chicken strips in the flour, dip into the eggs, and lastly roll the strips in the corn flakes. Place the strips on a wax paper–lined platter and refrigerate for 1 hour.

2 When you are ready to cook, heat the vegetable oil to 350°F in a medium skillet over medium-high heat. In batches, using tongs, carefully add the chicken strips to the oil and cook for 3 to 4 minutes per side or until golden brown and no longer pink in the center. Remove and place on a paper towel–lined platter to drain excess grease.

3 Cover loosely with aluminum foil to keep warm while preparing remaining batches. Serve with Double Dipping Sauce.

Makes 16 pieces

4 boneless, skinless chicken breast halves (about 1 pound), washed and patted dry

1 teaspoon Get 'Em Girl Essential Seasoning (page 16)

½ cup all-purpose flour

2 eggs, lightly beaten

2½ cups corn flakes, crushed

½ teaspoon salt

½ teaspoon ground black pepper

½ cup vegetable oil

½ cup mayonnaise

2 tablespoons honey

2 teaspoons yellow mustard

3 tablespoons extra virgin olive oil

1½ teaspoons Worcestershire sauce

3 tablespoons chili sauce

2 tablespoons ketchup

1 tablespoon water

½ teaspoon ground black pepper

¼ teaspoon sweet paprika

¼ teaspoon red pepper sauce

1 small onion, grated

1 teaspoon garlic paste

Double Dipping Sauce

*t*his sauce is perfect with our chicken fingers. We call it Double Dipping Sauce because after people have dipped once, they'll try and dip again . . . be warned!

Combine all ingredients in a small bowl; cover with plastic wrap and refrigerate until ready to serve.

Makes 2 cups

Pigs in a Blanket

a classic finger food that is perfect for birthdays, game day, or just as a snack.

1 Preheat the oven to 375°F.

2 Unroll the dough and separate into strips. Cut each strip into two 3-inch-long strips. Brush each strip lightly with honey mustard and top with one cocktail frank or one hot dog piece. Wrap the dough around each frank; pinch together at the seams to seal. Place seam side down, about 1 inch apart, on an ungreased baking sheet.

3 Bake until golden brown, about 15 minutes. Serve with additional honey mustard, for dipping.

Makes 24 pieces

One 11-ounce can refrigerated breadsticks

½ cup honey mustard

One 12- to 14-ounce package skinless cocktail franks (24) or 16-ounce package regular skinless hot dogs cut into 24 1-inch pieces

Grilled PB&J Cut-Out Sandwiches

Tools needed: 3-inch cookie cutters in kid-friendly shapes

¼ cup creamy peanut butter

20 slices whole-wheat bread, cut into fun shapes

⅛ cup strawberry jelly or jam

8 tablespoons (1 stick) unsalted butter, melted

Cinnamon-sugar blend

Ice-cold milk, for serving

*t*his is an adaptation of a sandwich that I first fell in love with as a child and then paid $9.50 for in a midtown Manhattan bakery (I know—crazy, right?). What child doesn't love peanut butter and jelly? Just make sure none of the children have peanut allergies and everything will be fine! —*Jeniece*

1 Spray a griddle or large skillet with nonstick cooking spray and heat it over medium-high heat.

2 Spread peanut butter on one side of 10 slices of bread and jelly on one side of the other 10 slices. Press together firmly to seal. With a pastry brush, lightly brush melted butter on one side of the sandwich.

3 Place the sandwich, buttered sided down, onto the hot griddle. Lightly brush the melted butter on the top. Cook for 2 minutes. Flip. Cook for another 2 minutes or until golden brown and heated through. Remove and sprinkle with the cinnamon-sugar blend. Serve immediately with ice-cold milk.

Makes 10 sandwiches

½ cup sugar

2 tablespoons ground cinnamon

Cinnamon-Sugar Blend

Blend the cinnamon and sugar together and store in an airtight jar. Sprinkle as desired atop your favorite desserts.

Makes ½ cup.

Veggie Bites with Buttermilk Ranch Dip

*a*delicious and easy way to get some vegetables in your kids' diet.

Mash the garlic and salt to a paste using the side of a chef's knife. In a medium bowl, whisk together the garlic paste, mayonnaise, sour cream, buttermilk, lemon juice, parsley, and scallions. Season with black pepper. Transfer to a serving bowl, arrange vegetables on a platter, and serve immediately.

Makes 2 cups dip; makes 6 to 8 servings

1 clove garlic

½ teaspoon kosher salt

1 cup mayonnaise

1 cup sour cream

½ cup buttermilk

Juice of ½ lemon

3 tablespoons minced fresh parsley

3 tablespoons minced scallions (white and green parts)

Ground black pepper

4 celery ribs, cut into 4-inch-long sticks

2 cups baby carrots

1 cup cherry tomatoes

Shakara's Fruit Punch

2 cups water

2 cups sugar

2 quarts cranberry juice concentrate

One 46-oz can pineapple juice

Two 6-ounce cans orange juice concentrate, thawed

2 oranges, cut into wedges

2 apples, cubed

Bring water and sugar to a boil in a heavy saucepan. Boil until sugar is dissolved, stirring occasionally, about 5 minutes. Let cool. Once cooled, add the fruit juices and fruits. Serve over ice.

Makes 1 gallon or sixteen 8-oz servings

DIY (Decorate It Yourself) Yellow Cupcakes with Easy Buttercream Frosting

*C*upcakes are the new black! Really, we love cupcakes—they are simple and easy to make, easily transported, and mess-free!

1 Preheat the oven to 325°F. Line two 12-cup muffin pans with paper cupcake liners.

2 Combine the flour, baking powder, salt, sugar, butter, eggs, half-and-half, and vanilla in a large bowl. Mix with an electric mixer on medium speed, scraping down the sides of the bowl with a silicone spatula, until well blended, about 45 seconds. Increase the mixer speed to high and continue to beat until the batter is smooth, about 3 minutes. Pour the batter into the prepared muffin pan cups, filling each three-quarters of the way. (You may only have enough batter for 20 cups.)

3 Bake until a wooden skewer inserted in the center of a cupcake comes out clean, about 20 minutes. Remove the cupcakes from the pans and cool completely on a wire rack.

4 For the frosting: Beat the butter, confectioners' sugar, and vanilla together in a large bowl with an electric mixer on medium speed. Add the half-and-half and blend until smooth.

5 Use a small offset metal spatula to frost the cupcakes with the buttercream frosting.

6 To serve: Set out the cupcakes on trays, cupcake trees, or cake plates along with bowls of colored sugar, sprinkles, chocolate morsels, and more.

Makes 20 cupcakes

CUPCAKES

2 cups all-purpose flour

3½ teaspoons baking powder

1 teaspoon salt

1½ cups granulated sugar

8 tablespoons (1 stick) unsalted butter, softened

3 large eggs

1 cup half-and-half

1 tablespoon vanilla extract

EASY BUTTERCREAM FROSTING

½ pound (2 sticks) unsalted butter, softened

3 cups confectioners' sugar

1 teaspoon vanilla extract

2 tablespoons half-and-half

Decorations, including colored sugar, sprinkles, chocolate morsels, etc.

Sausage and Pepperoni Pizza Tarts

2 tablespoons extra virgin olive oil

¼ pound (about 2 to 3 links) sweet Italian turkey sausage, removed from the casing

One 13.8-ounce tube refrigerated pizza dough (recommended: Pillsbury)

1½ cups marinara sauce (homemade or store-bought)

½ cup grated mozzarella cheese

¼ cup freshly grated Parmesan cheese

One 8-ounce package pepperoni slices

1 Preheat the oven to 350°F. Spray two 12-cup muffin pans with non-stick cooking spray.

2 Heat the olive oil in a medium skillet over medium heat. Add the sausage to the pan and cook, breaking up with the back of a wooden spoon, until no pink remains. Using a slotted spoon, transfer the sausage to a small bowl.

3 Lightly flour a clean work surface or cutting board and roll the pizza dough out to ⅛ inch thick. Cut out the dough into 24 2-inch circles and pat into the bottom and up the sides of the muffin pan cups.

4 Spread 1 to 2 teaspoons of marinara sauce onto the pizza dough. Top with mozzarella and Parmesan cheeses, and add the sausage and pepperoni.

5 Bake until the crust is golden brown and the cheese has melted, about 10 minutes. To serve, carefully remove tarts from the pan with a butter knife and place on a platter.

Makes 24 tarts

Macaroni and Cheese Bites

*W*e first tried these at a restaurant in Harlem, and quite frankly, we didn't enjoy them. The concept was great, but the end result was off. So we took it, added our own Get 'Em Girl twist—and our results turned out much better!

1 Line a baking sheet with parchment paper. Using a 2-inch scoop or a large melon baller, scoop out bite-size pieces of macaroni and cheese onto a large platter and set aside.

2 Mix together the flour, cayenne, if using, salt, and pepper in a shallow dish. In a separate dish, mix together the eggs and water. Place the bread crumbs in a third dish.

3 Roll each macaroni and cheese bite in the flour mixture, dip into the egg mixture, and finally roll in the bread crumbs. Place the bites on the baking sheet and refrigerate for 30 minutes to set.

4 Pour about 3 inches of oil in a heavy large saucepan and heat to 350°F.

5 In batches, carefully drop the bites into the oil and fry until golden brown, about 4 minutes. Remove with a slotted spoon to a paper towel–lined platter to drain any excess oil. Serve hot.

Makes about 30 bites

1 recipe Four-Cheese Macaroni and Cheese with a Kick! (page 157), refrigerated overnight

1½ cups all-purpose flour

¼ teaspoon cayenne pepper (optional)

½ teaspoon salt

½ teaspoon ground black pepper

2 large eggs

¼ cup water

1 cup panko or Japanese-style bread crumbs

Vegetable oil, for deep-frying

Chocolate Bonbons

6 cream-filled chocolate sandwich cookies, halved, with cream discarded (recommended: Oreos)

1 pint vanilla ice cream

26 ounces semisweet chocolate, chopped

1 tablespoon vegetable shortening

*t*hese are absolutely sinful—and so easy to make, you'll have to force yourself not to make them every day.

1 Set a wire rack over a baking sheet. Arrange the cookies, top side down, on the rack. Using a 2-inch ice cream scoop, scoop a ball of ice cream onto each cookie. Freeze for about 20 minutes, until hard.

2 In the top of a double boiler or a heatproof glass bowl set over a pot of simmering water, melt the chocolate and shortening together, stirring frequently. Remove from the heat and allow to cool slightly.

3 Remove the baking sheet from the freezer. Spoon the melted chocolate over the bonbons, making sure to cover them completely. Return the baking sheet to the freezer and allow to harden for at least 30 minutes, preferably overnight.

4 When ready to serve, remove from the freezer and serve immediately.

Makes 12 bonbons

Fight Night Bash

Heavyweight Bout
Philly Cheesesteak Pinwheels
Twice-Baked Potato Skins with Bacon and Sour Cream
Grown Folks Only Peach Iced Tea
Fried Apple Hand Pies

Middleweight Bout
Beer-Batter Shrimp with Spicy Tartar Sauce
Pulled Chicken Sandwiches with Easy Creamy Coleslaw
Gold Rush
Lip-Puckering Lemonade
Southern Girl Sweet Tea
Triple Chocolate Brownies

Welterweight Bout
Lemony Chicken Skewers
Sausage-Stuffed Mushrooms
Cranberry-Pineapple Punch

*n*ever let it be said that the Get 'Em Girls do not know how to throw a fight party. Our most memorable one would have to be the Trinidad versus Jones fight. Our friend, Don, was gracious enough to let us throw the party at his beautiful home. Don is notorious for throwing great parties, so his first question was do we have a DJ. Always being two steps ahead, we had already contacted our friends over at Digiwaxx because they always hook us up with the hottest DJs.

Once we got the location and music squared away, our next task was to get the word out. We were big fans of the movie *House Party*, so we expressed that to our web designer and he designed a hot e-mail blast reminiscent of the movies' promotional advertisements. Last but not least was the food and drinks. No party is complete without the two and we definitely had that covered with a menu that included sliders, jerk chicken wings, and caramel-pecan monkey bread as well as Joan's sneakily delicious hunch punch! We had over 100 of our friends attend — the party was fantastic, the food was a hit, and the music was great.

Here are some tips for throwing a great fight party:

Space

Living in New York City, space is always a consideration for us. When planning your fight party, make sure your guests can watch the fight comfortably. There is nothing worse than attending a fight party and missing the knockout punch because you could not see the television.

Food Selections

Be sure to choose your food selections wisely. If your food requires you to be in the kitchen throughout the evening, how can you enjoy yourself? Plan ahead and make sure the majority of your food is ready before your guests begin walking through the door and then you will have a better chance of preserving your sexy. Because at the end of the day it is all about the sexy—you didn't know?

Clean-Up Crew

Do not wait—let us repeat, do *not* wait—until the last guest has walked out the door to start cleaning up. Enlist your closest friends to help you pick up trash throughout the night—your feet will thank you.

Philly Cheesesteak Pinwheels

2 pounds skirt steak, trimmed of fat

Salt and ground black pepper

1 tablespoon unsalted butter

2 tablespoons extra virgin olive oil

1 large onion, thinly sliced

1 large green bell pepper, thinly sliced

1 clove garlic, minced

6 slices provolone cheese, sliced

8 to 10 6-inch wooden skewers, soaked in water

*i*nspired by one of our favorite cities and sandwiches!

1 Preheat a grill pan to medium-high. Place the steak between two large pieces of plastic wrap and pound the steak out with the flat side of a meat mallet until the steak is ¼ inch thick and 8 to 10 inches long. Season both sides of the steak with salt and pepper and set aside.

2 Melt the butter with the olive oil in a medium skillet over medium heat. Add the onions and green peppers and season with salt and pepper. Cook, stirring occasionally, for 7 minutes. Add the garlic to the pan and cook until the onions are soft and brown, about 3 minutes.

3 Lay the cheese lengthwise down the middle of the steak. Top with the onion and pepper mixture. Starting at one edge of the long side, begin tightly rolling the steak away from you. Insert skewers 1 inch apart through the roll, close to the overlapping edge, to hold the roll together; you should have 8 to 10 skewers inserted into the roll. Cut in between the skewers.

4 Spray a grill pan with nonstick cooking spray and heat it over medium-high heat. Grill the pinwheels cut-side down for 3 to 4 minutes per side for medium rare, or until your desired doneness.

Makes 8 to 10 pinwheels

Twice-Baked Potato Skins with Bacon and Sour Cream

1 Preheat the oven to 450°F. Arrange the potatoes on a baking sheet and bake until soft, about 45 minutes.

2 Meanwhile, cook the bacon in a large skillet over medium heat until crisp. Reserving the bacon drippings in the pan, drain the bacon on a paper towel–lined platter, and crumble. Add the red onion to the same skillet and cook until tender, about 5 minutes.

3 Remove the potatoes from the oven and let cool. Turn the oven up to 500°F. Once cool enough to handle, cut potatoes in half lengthwise and scoop out half of the flesh into a medium bowl. Reserve the potato skins. Mash together the potato flesh with the butter and heavy cream. Mix the cheddar and Monterey Jack together in a small bowl and add half to the potato mixture. Stir the bacon and onions into the potato mixture and season with salt and pepper.

4 Place the potato skins back onto the baking sheet, cut side up. Spoon the potato filling back into the potato skins and top each with the remainder of the cheese. Place back into the oven and bake until the cheese is melted and the potato skins are crisp, about 15 minutes. Remove and serve with a dollop of sour cream and a sprinkle of chives on top of each potato.

Makes 10 skins

5 large unpeeled Russet potatoes, washed and scrubbed

½ pound bacon

1 large red onion, chopped

4 tablespoons (½ stick) unsalted butter

¼ cup heavy cream

1 cup shredded cheddar cheese

1 cup shredded Monterey Jack cheese

Salt and ground black pepper

1 cup sour cream

5 tablespoons minced chives

Grown Folks Only Peach Iced Tea

4 cups cold water

6 orange pekoe tea bags

½ cup sugar

1½ cups peach nectar

1 cup Southern Comfort

Ice cubes

Peach slices, for garnish

In a medium saucepan, bring the water to a boil. Remove from heat, add the tea bags, and let steep for 10 minutes. Remove the tea bags (do not squeeze—it makes the tea bitter) and stir in the sugar until dissolved. Transfer the tea to a heat-safe pitcher and stir in the nectar. Place in the refrigerator to cool. Stir in the Southern Comfort before serving. Serve in a glass filled with ice and garnish each glass with a peach slice.

Makes 8 servings

Fried Apple Hand Pies

*t*he use of refrigerated pie dough makes this recipe super simple and quick to make. However, you can also use our recipe for Flaky Double Pie Crust on page 184.

1 Toss the apples with the lemon juice and set aside. In a small bowl, combine the cinnamon, nutmeg, and brown sugar. Stir the brown sugar mixture and the cornstarch into the apples and toss to coat.

2 Heat vegetable oil in a large heavy pot to 360°F.

3 Roll out the pie crusts on a lightly floured work surface and cut into twelve 3-inch circles using a cookie cutter or the rim of a glass dipped in flour. Put about 2 tablespoons of apple pie filling into the center of each round and fold the dough over. Crimp the edges together with a fork and cut two vents in the top of each pie to release the steam.

4 Fry the pies two at a time until golden brown, about 3 minutes. Remove with a slotted spoon and drain on a paper towel–lined platter. Sprinkle with confectioners' sugar and allow them to cool slightly before serving.

Makes 12 pies

4 Granny Smith apples, peeled, cored, and diced into ¼-inch cubes

Juice of ½ lemon

½ teaspoon ground cinnamon

¼ teaspoon freshly grated nutmeg

½ cup light brown sugar

2 teaspoons cornstarch

Vegetable oil, for deep frying

One 15-ounce package refrigerated pie crusts (recommended: Pillsbury)

1 cup confectioners' sugar

Beer-Batter Shrimp with Spicy Tartar Sauce

½ cup plus 2 tablespoons all-purpose flour

½ cup beer

2 tablespoons cold water

24 uncooked large shrimp, peeled and deveined (leave tails attached)

Vegetable oil, for deep frying

Spicy Tartar Sauce (recipe follows), for serving

*W*hether you are hosting a fight party or a surf and turf dinner for two, this dish is definitely the answer.

1 In a medium bowl, stir ½ cup of the flour with the beer and cold water until combined well. Set aside the batter for 30 minutes to rest.

2 When ready to cook, heat 3 inches of oil in a deep-fryer or large heavy pot to 350°F. Toss the shrimp with the remaining 2 tablespoons flour in a large bowl. A few shrimp at a time, shake off any excess flour and dip the shrimp into the batter. Carefully drop into the hot oil. Fry until lightly golden and crisp, 2 to 3 minutes. Remove with a slotted spoon to a paper towel–lined platter to drain. Serve immediately with spicy tartar sauce or your choice of condiments.

Makes 24 shrimp

1 cup mayonnaise

2 tablespoons sweet pickle relish

1 tablespoon minced onion

1 tablespoon fresh lemon juice

One 7-ounce can chipotle peppers in adobo sauce

Spicy Tartar Sauce

In a medium bowl, whisk together the mayonnaise, relish, onion, and lemon juice: starting with one chipotle, mince finely and stir into the mayonnaise mixture until well combined. Transfer to a serving dish.

Makes about 1 cup

Get 'Em Girl Essential Barbecue Rub

*W*hether you're a wet- or a dry-rub type of person, this mixture of spices is set to become as essential to your summer barbecue as a deck of cards!

Combine all ingredients in a small bowl and mix well. Will store for up to 6 months in a jar with a tight-fitting lid.

Makes about ¼ cup

2 tablespoons Spanish paprika

2 teaspoons chili powder

2 tablespoons kosher salt

2 teaspoons cumin

2 teaspoons sugar

2 tablespoons light brown sugar

1 teaspoon dry mustard

1 teaspoon ground black pepper

½ teaspoon dried thyme

½ teaspoon dried oregano

½ teaspoon cayenne pepper

1 teaspoon onion powder

2 teaspoons garlic powder

Pulled Chicken Sandwiches
with Easy Creamy Coleslaw

2 pounds boneless, skinless chicken thighs

Juice of 1 lemon

2 tablespoons Get 'Em Girl Essential Barbecue Rub (page 35)

1 cup Jeniece's Barbecue Sauce (page 76)

8 sandwich rolls, split and lightly toasted

16 dill pickle chips

Easy Creamy Coleslaw (recipe follows), for serving

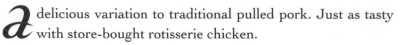

a delicious variation to traditional pulled pork. Just as tasty with store-bought rotisserie chicken.

1 Spray a grill or grill pan with nonstick cooking spray and preheat to medium-high heat.

2 Clean and rinse the chicken under cold running water and place in a large bowl. Pour the lemon juice over the chicken and let sit for 1 minute. Rinse well under cold water and pat dry with paper towels. Rub the chicken with the Barbecue Rub and grill, covered, turning occasionally, until the juices run clear and the chicken reaches an internal temperature of 180°F on an instant-read thermometer, about 25 to 30 minutes. Remove and let rest for 5 minutes before shredding the chicken with two forks.

3 Stir the chicken into the barbecue sauce in a large skillet. Cook until heated through, about 2 minutes, and serve on the rolls topped with pickles and coleslaw.

Makes 8 servings

---

1 medium head green cabbage, quartered, cored, and finely shredded

2 large carrots, finely shredded

1 cup mayonnaise

2 tablespoons sugar

2 tablespoons distilled white vinegar

1 tablespoon dry mustard

1½ teaspoons celery salt

¼ teaspoon salt

¼ teaspoon ground black pepper

Easy Creamy Coleslaw

Combine the cabbage and carrots in a large bowl. In a small bowl, whisk together the mayonnaise, sugar, vinegar, mustard, celery salt, salt, and pepper. Pour over the cabbage mixture. Toss to coat and adjust seasoning if necessary.

Makes 8 servings

Gold Rush

*t*his refreshing drink is great to have on sunny days while relaxing on your patio with friends.

Pour all ingredients into a large pitcher and stir well. Chill the mixture in the refrigerator for 1 hour.

Makes about 3 quarts

4 cups Lip-Puckering Lemonade (page 38)

4 cups Southern Girl Sweet Tea (page 39)

1 cup peach schnapps (recommended: DeKuyper's)

2 cups coconut-flavored rum

Lip-Puckering Lemonade

Juice of 8 large lemons, about
1 cup

1 cup granulated sugar, or to taste

7 cups cold water

In a large pitcher, combine the lemon juice and sugar, stirring continuously to dissolve sugar. Add the cold water and blend well.

Makes about 2 quarts

Southern Girl Sweet Tea

1 Place tea bags and baking soda in a 1-quart measuring cup. Pour boiling water over the tea bags. Cover and steep for 15 minutes.

2 Remove tea bags (do not squeeze). Pour tea into a 2-quart pitcher.

3 Stir in sugar until completely dissolved. Add cold water; refrigerate until chilled.

Makes about 2 quarts

6 orange pekoe tea bags

⅛ teaspoon baking soda

2 cups boiling water

1½ cups sugar

6 cups cold water

Triple Chocolate Brownies

4 ounces bittersweet chocolate, chopped

½ cup semisweet chocolate chips

1 ounce unsweetened chocolate, chopped

8 tablespoons (1 stick) unsalted butter

3 tablespoons cocoa powder

2 tablespoons instant coffee powder

3 large eggs

1½ cups granulated sugar

2 teaspoons vanilla extract

1 cup all-purpose flour

½ teaspoon salt

2 teaspoons confectioners' sugar, for garnish

*W*hen we first tested these brownies, we took them down to Mosaic Cuts, our neighborhood barbershop—and the shop shut down! Everyone loved the melt-in-your-mouth goodness of these decadent brownies. Enjoy!

1 Preheat the oven to 350°F. Line the bottom and sides of an 8-inch square baking pan with parchment paper and spray with nonstick cooking spray.

2 Melt the bittersweet chocolate, chocolate chips, and unsweetened chocolate with the butter in a double boiler or a medium heatproof glass bowl set over a pan of simmering water, stirring occasionally until smooth. Whisk in the cocoa powder and instant coffee. Set aside to cool.

3 In a small bowl, whisk together the eggs, sugar, and vanilla. Stir into the cooled chocolate mixture. Stir the flour and salt together in another small bowl and fold into the chocolate mixture with a silicone spatula until combined. Pour into the prepared pan and smooth the top with the spatula.

4 Bake until a wooden skewer inserted into the center comes out with very little crumbs, about 30 minutes. Remove from the oven and cool slightly in the pan. When ready to serve, turn out the brownies onto a platform, cut into squares, and dust with confectioners' sugar.

Makes 9 brownies

Lemony Chicken Skewers

1 Place the chicken in a resealable plastic bag. Whisk together the olive oil, garlic, lemon juice and peel, parsley, thyme, and salt and pepper, and pour over the chicken. Seal the bag and marinate in the refrigerator for 8 hours.

2 When ready to cook, heat an outdoor grill or grill pan to medium. Thread the chicken pieces onto the skewers. (Discard the marinade.) Grill until cooked through, about 10 to 15 minutes, turning occasionally.

Makes 15 skewers

1½ pounds chicken breast tenders (about 15 pieces)

½ cup extra virgin olive oil

2 cloves garlic, minced

Juice and grated peel of 2 lemons

2 tablespoons chopped flat-leaf parsley

Leaves from 1 sprig thyme (about ¼ teaspoon), chopped

Salt and ground black pepper

15 7-inch wood skewers, soaked in water

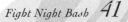

Sausage-Stuffed Mushrooms

Extra virgin olive oil

24 large white mushrooms

½ teaspoon salt

1 pound sweet Italian turkey sausage, removed from casing

2 cloves garlic, minced

¼ teaspoon ground black pepper

¼ cup finely chopped flat-leaf parsley

½ cup freshly grated Parmesan cheese

½ cup Italian-style bread crumbs

*t*his recipe is definitely one of my favorite entertaining dishes. Your guest will enjoy the savory taste. —*Joan*

1 Preheat the oven to 375°F. Drizzle the bottom of a large casserole dish with olive oil and set aside.

2 Wipe off the mushrooms with a clean damp kitchen towel. Remove the stems and reserve. Place the mushroom caps in the casserole, drizzle with olive oil, and season with ¼ teaspoon salt.

3 Heat 3 tablespoons olive oil in a large skillet over medium heat. Finely chop the mushroom stems and add them to the skillet along with the sausage, garlic, and the remaining salt and pepper. Cook, breaking up the sausage with the back of a wooden spoon, just until browned. Remove from the heat and stir in the parsley and ¼ cup of the Parmesan.

4 In a small bowl, mix the remaining cheese with the bread crumbs. Generously fill the mushrooms with the sausage mixture. Sprinkle the tops with the bread crumb mixture and drizzle with olive oil.

5 Bake until the stuffing is browned and the mushrooms are soft, about 20 minutes.

Makes 24 mushrooms

Cranberry-Pineapple Punch

Combine cranberry juice, pineapple juice, and sugar in a large pitcher. Mix until sugar dissolves. Refrigerate. Add the ginger ale just before serving.

Makes 2 quarts

2 cups cranberry juice cocktail

2 cups pineapple juice

¾ cup sugar

1 liter ginger ale

"Girls' Bite In" Slumber Party

Ladies' Night Menu
Evening

Diva Supreme Pizza

Mesclun Salad with Dijon Vinaigrette

Chocolate Bread Pudding with White Chocolate Ganache

Cocoa Cure Chocolate Martinis (page 197)

Good Morning Divas
Morning

Rise-and-Shine Breakfast Smoothies

Cinnamon-Raisin Scones

Apple-Cinnamon Oatmeal with Brown Sugar Cream

NOLA-Style Beignets

Farmhouse Cheddar Breakfast Burritos

When is the last time you got together with your closest girlfriends for a slumber party? If you are anything like us, it's probably been a while. Yes, we get together for all nighters—but trust us, there's no partying involved! So one evening we decided to put our ideas on hold and just relax. No work—just laughs, food, drinks, and Brick Breaker battles! That evening led to this section.

If you can, send the kids to your parents, your husband to his brother's house, and allow yourself one evening with a few of your closest girlfriends to reconnect, recharge, and relive the days when all that mattered was who would fall asleep first and how she would be punished. The presentation due first thing Monday morning will still be there; the dog will still need to go to the groomer; and you will still need to pick up your suit from the cleaners before Sunday—but you've got 24 hours before any of that will matter again!

Below are a few ideas to make your "Girls' Bite In" Slumber Party a success.

Chick Flicks

There are certain movies that we can't get enough of. Here are some of our favorites: *Love Jones, Love & Basketball, Last Holiday, Dream Girls, Waiting to Exhale, How Stella Got Her Groove Back, Pretty Woman, Something New*, and *You've Got Mail*.

Get-to-Know-You Games

Just when you thought you knew . . . you had no idea! That is, until you played that game of truth or dare or when you got alcohol poisoning during a game of I Never.

Makeover Session

Have your girlfriends bring over their favorite beauty products and share. Give each other facial scrubs, manicures, and pedicures, and don't forget to share your favorite makeup, beauty tips, and secrets while sipping martinis.

Diva Supreme Pizza

2 tablespoons unsalted butter

¼ cup extra virgin olive oil

2 large yellow onions, thinly sliced

Salt

½ teaspoon sugar

1 pound pizza dough (store-bought or homemade)

½ cup ricotta cheese, drained

2 cups grated mozzarella cheese

3 tablespoons freshly grated Parmesan cheese

2 cups shredded cooked chicken

Ground black pepper

4 fresh basil leaves, cut into thin strips

We had a get-together at Jeniece's apartment to welcome our friend Eric into the family, and this pizza was on the menu. Make it your own by adding whatever toppings you prefer. We didn't have the time to make the pizza dough, so we stopped at our local pizzeria and purchased a ball of dough, but if you prefer to make your own, please do so.

1 Preheat the oven to 400°F.

2 In a large skillet, melt the butter with 2 tablespoons of the olive oil over medium heat. Add the onions and sprinkle with 1 teaspoon salt. Cook, stirring constantly, until the onions begin to brown and soften, about 10 minutes. Reduce the heat to low and sprinkle onions with the sugar; continue to cook, stirring occasionally, until the onions are well browned and soft, about 30 minutes.

3 Meanwhile, roll out the pizza dough to fit a 12-inch pizza pan that has been sprayed with nonstick cooking spray. Lift and pinch the edge of the dough to form a lip. Drizzle the pizza dough with the remaining olive oil and spread the ricotta cheese on top. Sprinkle the mozzarella and Parmesan across the top. Top with the onions and chicken. Season with salt and pepper and top with the basil.

4 Bake until the crust is brown and the cheese is bubbly, about 30 minutes. Serve hot.

Makes one 12-inch pizza

Mesclun Salad with Dijon Vinaigrette

*t*he perfect starter dish. If you can't find mesclun salad mix, choose your favorite mix of young lettuces and greens.

In a small bowl, whisk together the olive oil, mustard, vinegar, and black pepper until well combined. Place the mesclun greens and tomatoes in a large bowl and drizzle liberally with vinaigrette. Toss to coat, top with Parmesan cheese, and serve immediately. Place the remaining vinaigrette in an airtight jar and refrigerate for up to 1 week.

Makes 2 cups dressing; makes 4 to 6 servings

1¼ cups extra virgin olive oil

⅓ cup Dijon mustard

⅓ cup red wine vinegar

¼ teaspoon ground black pepper

12 ounces mesclun greens, washed and dried thoroughly

1 cup halved cherry tomatoes

¼ **cup freshly grated Parmesan cheese**

Chocolate Bread Pudding with White Chocolate Ganache

1¾ cups heavy cream

¾ cup sugar

¼ cup whole milk

1¼ cups semisweet chocolate chips

1 large egg

1 teaspoon vanilla extract

1 loaf French bread or baguette with crust, cut into ½-inch pieces

White Chocolate Ganache (recipe follows)

*W*e shared this decadent dessert while in New Orleans, and we must tell you, we fought so badly over the last spoonful that we had to come back and re-create it.

1 Preheat the oven to 300°F.

2 In a heavy-bottomed medium saucepan, bring the cream, ½ cup of the sugar, and the milk to a simmer over low heat. Simmer, stirring constantly, until the sugar dissolves. Remove the pan from the heat and add 1 cup of the chocolate chips, whisking constantly until melted and smooth.

3 In a large bowl, whisk together the egg and vanilla; slowly whisk about ¼ cup of the chocolate mixture into the egg mixture, to warm the egg. When the mixture is smooth, slowly whisk in the remaining chocolate mixture. Set aside to cool slightly.

4 Using a silicone spatula, fold the bread cubes and the remaining chocolate chips into the custard, making sure to combine well. Transfer to an 8-inch square baking dish and sprinkle the top with the remaining ¼ cup of sugar.

5 Bake until the custard is thickened and the center is set, about 1 hour. Serve warm, drizzled with white chocolate ganache.

Makes 6 to 8 servings

1½ cups heavy cream

8 ounces white chocolate chips

White Chocolate Ganache

In a heavy-bottomed medium saucepan, bring the cream to a simmer over medium-low heat. Remove from the heat. Place the white chocolate chips in a medium heatproof bowl and pour the cream over them. Let sit for 1 minute, then whisk until smooth. Transfer to a serving dish and drizzle over each portion of bread pudding.

Makes 2 cups

Rise-and-Shine Breakfast Smoothies

i love drinking this smoothie for breakfast; it gives me the boost of energy I need to get up and out in the morning.

—Joan

Combine all the ingredients in a blender. Blend on high speed until smooth, about 45 seconds. Serve immediately

Makes 2 servings

1 large ripe banana, sliced

1 cup strawberries, hulled

½ cup raspberries

1 cup plain yogurt

¼ cup orange juice

2 tablespoons honey

Cinnamon-Raisin Scones

3 cups plus 1 tablespoon
all-purpose flour

1 tablespoon baking powder

3½ teaspoons ground cinnamon

½ pound (2 sticks) unsalted butter,
softened

¼ cup plus 2 tablespoons sugar

3 large eggs

⅓ cup heavy cream

⅓ cup raisins

Honey Butter (page 121),
for serving

Preserves, for serving

1 Preheat the oven to 350°F. Line a baking sheet with parchment paper.

2 Sift together 3 cups of the flour, the baking powder and 2 teaspoons of the cinnamon into a large bowl.

3 In another large bowl, with an electric mixer on medium, beat the butter until creamy. Add ¼ cup of the sugar and beat until fluffy and pale. One at a time, add the eggs, beating after each addition.

4 Slowly add the flour mixture and the cream. Mix just until blended.

5 In a small bowl, toss the raisins with the remaining tablespoon of flour. Fold into the batter. Using an ice cream scoop, place the dough on the baking sheet.

6 In a small bowl, mix together the remaining 1½ teaspoons of cinnamon and 2 tablespoons of sugar. Sprinkle the cinnamon-sugar mixture over each of the scones. Bake for 20 minutes, until golden brown. Serve warm with honey butter and preserves.

Makes 12 scones

Apple-Cinnamon Oatmeal with Brown Sugar Cream

*Y*ou will not be able to go back to eating an envelope pack of instant oatmeal again after you taste this one . . . We promise!

—Joan

1 In a medium saucepan, bring the water and milk to a boil. Stir in the oats and salt and cook a few minutes to thicken. Reduce the heat to low and stir in the applesauce and butter; simmer uncovered for 30 minutes, stirring occasionally.

2 Meanwhile, combine the cream, brown sugar, and cinnamon in a large bowl. Use a mixer with a whip attachment to whip until stiff. Cover the bowl with plastic wrap and refrigerate until ready to serve.

3 Serve the oatmeal hot in bowls with a dollop of the brown sugar cream in the center.

Makes 4 servings

1½ cups water

2 cups milk

1 cup quick-cooking oats (not instant)

Pinch of salt

½ cup applesauce

4 tablespoons (½ stick) unsalted butter

½ cup heavy cream

1 teaspoon light brown sugar

⅛ teaspoon cinnamon

NOLA-Style Beignets

1 package active dry yeast

¾ cup warm water (110°F)

¼ cup light brown sugar

½ teaspoon salt

1 large egg, beaten

½ cup evaporated milk

3¾ cups all-purpose flour

2 tablespoons vegetable shortening

Vegetable oil, for deep-frying

Confectioners' sugar, for serving

*W*e went to New Orleans two years ago for a book signing and completely fell in love with the beignets; now it's the first thing we get when we arrive to the N.O. —*Jeniece*

1 In a large bowl, combine the yeast, warm water, and brown sugar, and let the mixture sit for 5 minutes. Add the salt, egg, and milk, and mix on low speed with an electric mixer.

2 Slowly add half of the flour until the dough begins to come together. Add the shortening. When shortening is incorporated, add the remaining flour until most of it is incorporated.

3 Place the dough onto a floured work surface and knead the dough, adding just enough flour to make the dough nonsticky and smooth. Place the dough into a large oiled bowl, loosely cover, and let rise until dough has doubled in size, approximately 1 hour.

4 After the dough has doubled in size, punch it down. Turn it on a floured surface and roll out into a rectangle about ½ inch thick. Cut into 2-inch strips on a diagonal. Place the beignets on a floured baking sheet to let rise in a warm place about 40 minutes.

5 Heat 3 inches of vegetable oil in a large saucepan to 350°F. Place the beignets into the hot oil one at a time, being careful not to smash or deflate dough. Cook until they are golden brown on both sides, about 2 minutes per side. Remove and place on a paper towel–lined platter to drain. Cover beignets completely with confectioners' sugar and serve warm.

Makes about 24 beignets

Farmhouse Cheddar Breakfast Burritos

a simple breakfast burrito is taken to another level with the deliciousness that is farmhouse cheddar.

1 Whisk together the eggs, water, salt, and pepper in a medium bowl.

2 Melt the butter and olive oil in a medium skillet over medium-high heat and add the sausage. Cook, breaking up with the back of a wooden spoon, until no pink remains. Drain off the fat and stir in the egg mixture and the chives. Continue to cook, stirring often, until the eggs have set, about 40 seconds. Sprinkle with the cheese. Reduce the heat to low and place the flour tortillas on top of the burrito filling to warm slightly, about 30 seconds.

3 To assemble: Remove the skillet from the heat and place the tortillas on a flat surface. Top the tortillas evenly down the center with the egg and sausage filling. Roll up like a burrito. Serve seam side down, topped with the salsa.

Makes 2 servings

4 large eggs

1 tablespoon water

½ teaspoon salt

¼ teaspoon ground black pepper

1 tablespoon unsalted butter

1 tablespoon extra virgin olive oil

½ pound bulk breakfast sausage

1 tablespoon chopped chives

¼ cup grated farmhouse cheddar cheese (recommended: Artisanal Premium)

Two 8-inch flour tortillas

½ cup mild salsa

Poker Night ... with the Girls

Royal Flush
Sassy Girl Sliders
Crispy Baked Potato Wedges
Slow-Cooker Chili
Pears and Blue Cheese on Endive Spears

Full House
Danni's Honey Barbecue Wings
White Bean Dip with Pita Crisps
Cucumber and Dill Salad

So you've checked out a few episodes of *Celebrity Poker Showdown* and you are ready to take your friends for everything they're worth at the table. You've decided that you want to host a weekly poker night, so you run out and get everything you need: playing chips, a deck of cards, and your green visor. You exhaust your 401K and send invites to all your cronies letting them know it's going down! But before you jump into full Vegas mode, we've decided to break down the game just a bit, so you'll know when to hold 'em . . . and when to fold 'em!

Fortunately for you, there are more than a few variations of poker—easier to take your friends for everything they're worth, you say? Well, unfortunately, we're only covering the basic game of poker, better known as 5-Card Draw, so you are on your own from there.

Before you begin playing, all players should decide on a betting limit. Setting a betting limit will ensure that whoever came friends will leave friends. It will also prevent you from gambling away your baby's college fund! Now that we've got that out of the way . . . let's get to the rules.

To begin, each player will need to ante up. (Brooklyn readers, put your jewelry back on . . . we're talking about placing a bet.) There's no limit on the ante, but it should start with whatever your minimum bet is.

The dealer deals five cards facedown, clockwise around the table, starting with the player to the dealer's left, and making sure to always deal him or herself last. Once everyone has received their five cards, the remainder of the deck is placed facedown in the center of the table, and the game begins.

At this point, each player can now look at their cards to check out what they are working with. Generally, the round of betting starts with the player to the left of the dealer, with the remainder of the players following suit. During the first round of betting you only have a couple of options you can exercise. You can either *open* the bet, which simply means you place a starting bet, or *check* the bet, which is only allowed if no one has opened the bet yet and you don't want to start the betting . . . but are not ready to throw in the towel, either.

However, once a bet is made, you must either *see* (match) that bet or take it a step further and *raise* that bet. So, for instance, if you bet fifty cents (hey, there's nothing wrong with being frugal), in order for the next player to stay in the game, they would have to *see* your fifty-cent bet by putting in fifty cents of their own, or if they're feeling rather lucky, they could *raise* your bet by another fifty cents. At this point the next player could either *see* the now—one dollar bet or roll on out of this high-rolling hand. This brings us to the next option . . .

What did your mother teach you about being a quitter? If your lesson was anything like ours, you learned that quitting is for suckers . . . well, scrap that, because in the game of poker, baby, knowing when to *fold* (quit) can sometimes mean the difference between one broken leg or two! There is no right or wrong time to *fold*—in fact, you can *fold* as early as right after the first bet is made. Don't be ashamed—put those cards down and go grab yourself a hot wing!

Now that all the betting, checking, seeing, raising, and folding are done, those who are still left in the game have the option to trade in up to three cards for new ones, making sure to keep the cards traded in facedown on the table. Once everyone has thrown in and received their new cards, the betting, checking, seeing, raising, and folding begin again.

After the second round of betting is completed, the remaining players show their hands. The player with the highest hand wins the pot! Everybody else will rush the buffet of delicious dishes you've prepared, because they just lost this week's grocery money.

Cards and Their Values

Poker is played with a regular deck of 52 playing cards ranked from high to low: Ace, King, Queen, Jack, 10, 9, 8, 7, 6, 5, 4, 3, 2. The cards are also separated into four suits: clubs (black), spades (black), hearts (red), and diamonds (red). Now, we all know diamonds are a girl's best friend, but in this game, the suits are all of equal value, so chuck what you learned playing Spades or Hearts, ladies!

Winning Hands

The highest ranking hand wins the pot, and card hands are ranked in the following order from highest to lowest value:

Royal Flush: Five cards of the same suit in numerical order from 10 to Ace. This is the most valuable hand you can have—and the most difficult hand to get!—so if you get one, you're sitting pretty!

Straight Flush: Five cards of the same suit in numerical order. The cards can't "wrap around" (i.e., Q, K, A, 2, 3), and if there's a tie (two players both have straight flushes), the player with the highest card in her straight flush wins.

Four of a Kind: Four cards of equal rank (example: four Queens) and another unrelated card. If there's a tie, the player with the highest ranking four-of-a-kind wins.

Full House: Three cards of equal rank, plus two other cards of equal rank (example: three 7s and two 10s). If there's a tie, the player with the highest ranking three-card set wins.

Flush: Any five cards of the same suit, regardless of numerical order. If there's a tie, the player with the highest ranking card in her flush wins.

Straight: Five cards in numerical order, but not in the same suit. Like a straight flush, the cards can't wrap around (i.e., Q, K, A, 2, 3), and if there's a tie, the player with the highest ranking card in her straight wins.

Three of a Kind: Three cards of equal rank and two unrelated cards. If there's a tie, the player with the highest ranking set of three cards wins.

Two Pair: Two separate pairs of equal rank and another unrelated card (example: two 5s, two Jacks, and a 3). If there's a tie, the player with the highest ranking pair wins.

Pair: Two equal-value cards and three unrelated cards. If there's a tie, the player holding the highest ranking pair wins.

High Card: If no one has any of the nine hands listed above, the player holding the highest ranking card in her hand wins. If there's a tie for highest ranking card, the player holding the second-highest ranking card wins . . . and so on.

Sassy Girl Sliders

1½ pounds ground turkey

One 4-serving packet dry onion soup mix

¾ cup water

¼ teaspoon salt

¼ teaspoon ground black pepper

10 small potato rolls, split and lightly toasted

Condiments of your choice

*W*e made these for the fight party at our friend Don's house not too long ago and we don't know which went down faster, the sliders or Felix Trinidad! Might we suggest you double the recipe, just to be on the safe side?

1 In a large bowl, using your hands, mix together the ground turkey, onion soup mix, water, salt, and pepper; mix just until combined.

2 Using a ¼-cup measuring cup or a 2-ounce ice cream scoop, make 10 thin patties and place on a parchment paper–lined platter. Cover with plastic wrap and refrigerate for 30 minutes.

3 When ready to cook, spray a grill pan with nonstick cooking spray and heat over medium-high heat. Carefully place the patties in the pan, pressing down gently with a metal spatula. Cook until cooked through-out and no pink remains, about 3 minutes per side.

4 To assemble the sliders: Place the sliders in between the potato rolls and serve immediately with a choice of condiments.

Makes 10 sliders

MAKE IT
YOUR OWN

For a cheese slider, top the patties, after flipping once, with slices of mild cheddar cheese or any sliced cheese of your choice.

Crispy Baked Potato Wedges

Preheat the oven to 450°F. Cut each potato lengthwise into eight wedges; toss in a large bowl with the butter, olive oil, seasoned salt, and pepper. Arrange in a single layer on two baking sheets. Bake, turning potatoes halfway through baking, until fork tender and golden, about 45 minutes. Remove from oven, garnish with parsley, and serve immediately.

Makes 6 to 8 servings

8 large Russet potatoes, peeled

6 tablespoons (¾ stick) unsalted butter, melted

6 tablespoons extra virgin olive oil

1 tablespoon seasoned salt

½ teaspoon ground black pepper

1 teaspoon chopped fresh parsley, for garnish

Slow-Cooker Chili

2 pounds ground beef

3 tablespoons plus 2 teaspoons chili powder

One 15-ounce can red kidney beans, rinsed and drained

One 15-ounce can black beans, rinsed and drained

Two 28-ounce cans crushed tomatoes

One 15-ounce can low-sodium chicken broth

One 7-ounce can chipotle peppers in adobo sauce, chopped (use less if desired)

1½ teaspoons salt

1½ teaspoons onion powder

1 teaspoon granulated garlic

1 teaspoon dried oregano

1 teaspoon ground cumin

¼ teaspoon ground cinnamon

FOR SERVING

Blue and yellow corn chips

1 cup sour cream

½ cup grated cheddar cheese

½ cup Monterey Jack cheese

¼ cup chopped scallions

*t*his is the most convenient and multi-task-friendly dish ever; you can finish shopping, decorate, and put out the party favors while this chili is cooking.

1 Crumble the ground beef in the slow cooker and stir in 3 tablespoons of the chili powder, the beans, tomatoes, chicken broth, chipotles, salt, onion powder, garlic, oregano, cumin, and cinnamon. Cover and cook on the low setting for 6 hours.

2 When you are ready to serve, stir in the remaining 2 teaspoons of chili powder and season with additional salt and pepper if necessary. Serve the chili in warm bowls along with the corn chips and toppings of your choice.

Makes 6 to 8 servings

Pears and Blue Cheese on Endive Spears

1 Cook the butter, sugar, and pears together in a large skillet over medium heat, stirring occasionally, until the pears are soft and browned, about 8 minutes; remove from heat and set aside to cool.

2 In a medium bowl, whisk together the mayonnaise, lemon juice, and black pepper. Stir in the Gorgonzola and refrigerate until ready to use.

3 To assemble the spears, spread 1 tablespoon of Gorgonzola dressing inside each spear and top with pears. Top each spear with a pecan half and serve. Refrigerate remaining gorgonzola dressing in an airtight jar for up to 1 week.

Makes 12 spears

2 tablespoons unsalted butter

1½ teaspoons sugar

1 Bosc pear, peeled, cored, and diced

1 cup mayonnaise

1 tablespoon fresh lemon juice

½ teaspoon ground black pepper

1 cup crumbled Gorgonzola cheese

½ cup pecan halves, toasted

12 endive spears, washed and dried thoroughly

Danni's Honey Barbecue Wings

5 pounds chicken wings, disjointed and tips discarded

½ cup fresh lemon juice (about 5 lemons)

1 tablespoon Get 'Em Girl Essential Seasoning (page 16)

1½ teaspoons ground black pepper

3 tablespoons extra virgin olive oil

Vegetable oil, for deep frying

2 cups all-purpose flour

2 cups Simple Honey Barbecue Sauce (page 67)

*m*y junior year in high school, I hosted a sleepover, and my friend Danielle brought a pot of what we called honey barbecue wing soup. In fact, there was far more honey barbecue than wings. Let's just say the wings have come a very long way from our Bergtraum H.S. days—they are absolutely delicious now! Enjoy. —*Jeniece*

1 Clean and rinse chicken under cold running water. Place in a large bowl and add lemon juice, let sit for 1 minute, and rinse well with cold water. Pat dry with paper towels and place chicken in another large bowl.

2 In a small bowl, combine the Essential Seasoning, pepper, and olive oil. Pour over the chicken and toss to coat each piece. Cover bowl with plastic wrap and marinate in the refrigerator for 30 minutes.

3 When ready to cook, preheat the oven to 400°F. Heat about 3 inches of vegetable oil over high heat in a large skillet, preferably cast iron, until very hot but not smoking, about 350°F. While the oil is heating, place the flour in a resealable plastic bag. Add the chicken in batches to the flour and shake until chicken is completely coated.

4 In batches, carefully add the chicken to the skillet, making sure not to overcrowd the skillet. Fry chicken, uncovered, turning once with tongs, until golden brown on both sides and crisp, about 6 to 8 minutes. Remove the chicken from the skillet with a slotted spoon or skimmer and drain on a paper towel-lined platter. Transfer to a large baking sheet and cover loosely with aluminum foil while you prepare the rest of the chicken.

5 Once all of the chicken has been fried, toss the chicken with the honey barbecue sauce; transfer to another bowl if needed. Spread in an even layer onto two large baking sheets and continue cooking in the oven until the wings are crisp and sticky, about 30 minutes.

Makes about 10 servings

Simple Honey Barbecue Sauce

*t*his sauce is great for anyone who prefers their barbecue sauce with a little more sweet than heat. It's delicious on chicken wings and baby back ribs alike!

1 Combine all the ingredients in a medium pot over medium heat. Bring to a simmer, stirring occasionally, and reduce heat to low. Cook, uncovered, stirring often, until the sauce has thickened slightly and coats the back of a wooden spoon, about 20 to 25 minutes.

2 Remove from heat and use immediately or allow to cool completely and store in an airtight jar in the refrigerator for up to 5 days.

Makes about 2 cups

1¼ cups ketchup

½ cup honey

2 tablespoons brown sugar

1 tablespoon yellow mustard

2 tablespoons Worcestershire sauce

1½ teaspoons cider vinegar

1 teaspoon fresh lemon juice

1 teaspoon Get 'Em Girl Essential Seasoning (page 16)

¼ teaspoon salt

¼ teaspoon ground black pepper

¼ teaspoon garlic powder

¼ teaspoon onion powder

⅛ teaspoon ground cinnamon

½ teaspoon paprika

⅛ teaspoon ground ginger

⅛ teaspoon dried oregano

White Bean Dip with Pita Crisps

One 19-ounce can white kidney beans, rinsed and drained

2 small cloves garlic, peeled

¼ cup scallions, white and green parts, chopped

2 tablespoons fresh lemon juice

¼ teaspoon ground cumin

¼ teaspoon dried oregano

3 tablespoons extra virgin olive oil

Salt and ground black pepper

Place the beans, garlic, scallions, lemon juice, cumin, and oregano in the bowl of a food processor and process until smooth. Slowly add the olive oil until the hummus comes together. Season with salt and pepper and serve with pita crisps.

Makes about 7 servings

---

7 pita bread pockets

¼ cup extra virgin olive oil

½ teaspoon salt

¼ teaspoon ground black pepper

½ teaspoon dried basil

½ teaspoon dried oregano

Pita Crisps

1 Preheat the oven to 400°F.

2 Cut each pita bread into eight wedges. Arrange the pita wedges on a large baking sheet.

3 In a small bowl, combine the olive oil, salt, pepper, basil, and oregano, and generously brush each side of the pita wedges with the oil mixture.

4 Bake until toasted and golden brown, about 7 minutes. Remove and serve warm with the white bean dip.

Makes about 7 servings

Cucumber and Dill Salad

*t*his simple yet delicious salad is great as a quick side dish to any meal. Experiment with different herbs and ingredients to make it your own.

1 Combine the vinegar, water, sugar, salt, and pepper in a small pot over medium-low heat. Cook, stirring occasionally, until the sugar is completely dissolved. Remove from heat and cool slightly.

2 In a medium glass bowl, combine the cucumbers and onions. When the sugar mixture has cooled, pour the mixture over the cucumbers and onions, tossing to coat. Cover with plastic wrap and refrigerate for at least 1 hour. When ready to serve, stir in the fresh dill and tomatoes and serve immediately or store for up to 12 hours.

Serves 6 to 8

1 cup white vinegar

¾ cup water

¾ cup sugar

1 teaspoon salt

¼ teaspoon ground black pepper

3 large seedless or English cucumbers, cut into ¼-inch slices

1 large red onion, halved and thinly sliced

3 tablespoons chopped fresh dill

1½ cups halved cherry tomatoes

It's a Family Reunion

Isley Family Barbecue

Barbecue Baby Back Ribs
Bacon and Cheddar–Stuffed Burgers
Grilled Marinated Chicken
Uncle Larry's Fried Whiting
Jeniece's Baked Beans
Crystal's Macaroni Salad
Dirty, Dirty Rice
Devilish Eggs
Pomegranate Iced Tea with Simple Syrup
Strawberry Shortcake Trifle

Davis Family Barbecue

Caribbean Jerk Chicken
Spice-Rubbed Grilled Tilapia
Grilled Corn on the Cob with Smoked Bacon Butter
Joan's Honey Cornbread
Easy Creamy Coleslaw (page 36)
Red Bliss–Caesar Potato Salad
Lip-Puckering Strawberry Lemonade (page 143)
Spiked Fruit Salad

Bridgers Family Barbecue

Spicy Turkey Burgers
Hilton's Smoked Ribs
Honey Barbecue Chicken Quarters
Barbecue Shrimp Skewers
Sandra's Pasta and Seafood Salad
Strawberry Pudding
Frances B's Punch

*t*here is nothing like getting together with your family for good times. Everyone gathered in "the front room" looking at old photos, reminiscing about old times, family members who have passed on, and just having a beautiful time. There is a familiarity and closeness that you feel when you look over and see someone who has your nose; when you see the newest member of the family and he looks like your grandfather; or just knowing that you can be yourself with no pretense. So with this section, we wanted to celebrate the essence of family, with the family reunion.

When you think of family reunions, if you are not on the reunion committee, you think about a weekend of great company, delicious food, and fun! But, anyone who has ever had the pleasure (and pain) of putting together a family reunion knows all too well the headaches that can result from poor planning and organization, and mismanagement. We want to give you a few pointers and some delicious menu options from our very own families, which will help you in taking the first step to planning a successful family reunion.

Get organized!

Before you can even begin to go out and start planning your family's reunion, put together a list of tasks that need to be fulfilled. Understand that although this is a great cause, a reunion is hard work and can become overwhelming very quickly. You will need to contact family members, set a budget and track funds, appoint committee members, contract locations and rental equipment, and oversee the weekend's events to a T—so be prepared!

Ask for help!

Unless you work best on your own, it would be wise to contact other family members for help in putting together your reunion. Assign a committee to help with the responsibilities of the reunion planning. The following are a few of the committees we've used when planning our own family reunions.

Budget Committee: responsible for opening a bank account, tracking, and managing funds collected for reunion events and bills.

Communication Committee: maintains names and contact information for all relatives and is responsible for contacting relatives regarding reunion activities.

Food Committee: responsible for arranging the meals for the entire event, whether catered or homemade.

Welcome Committee: responsible for meeting and greeting all family members on the day of. Ideally, this committee should consist of members of the family who have stayed in frequent contact with extended family members, as well as someone who enjoys researching the family genealogy.

Last but not least, enjoy yourself!

We know it will be hard, but try and get a good night's sleep the evening before the event—it will definitely help! With making sure that everyone has tee shirts, the potato sack race starts on time, and a fight doesn't break out at the Spades table (listen, we're family, but renege and somebody is liable to leave with stitches!), you will need all the energy you can muster!

Get 'Em Girls' Top 5 Family Reunion Songs

1 "Family Reunion"—O'Jays
2 "Electric Slide"—Marcia Griffith
3 "We Are Family"—Sister Sledge
4 "Family Affair"—Sly and the Family Stone
5 "Before I Let You Go"—Maze featuring Frankie Beverly

Top 5 Things Overheard at the Family Reunion

1 "Who made the potato salad?"
2 "No talking across the board!"
3 "Whose child is that?"
4 "You sure I wasn't adopted?"
5 "This is my last family reunion!"

Barbecue Baby Back Ribs

*e*veryone has their own special recipe when preparing ribs; whether you are a dry rub or wet sauce person, these are as good as it gets — Get 'Em Girl style!

1 Trim the membrane from the back of each rack of ribs by running a paring knife between the membrane and the ribs; wash and pat dry with paper towels. Generously season the ribs with Essential Barbecue Rub and massage into the meat. Wrap each slab of ribs in heavy-duty aluminum foil and refrigerate for at least 8 hours.

2 When ready to cook, remove the ribs from the refrigerator, place on a baking sheet (still in the foil), and allow to come to room temperature while you preheat the oven to 250°F. Open the foil and brush each slab of ribs with Jeniece's Barbecue Sauce. Securely rewrap the ribs in the foil and place them in the oven. Bake for 2½ hours.

3 After 2½ hours, turn on the broiler to high, open the foil, and place the ribs under the broiler, just until the sauce begins to caramelize, 5 to 7 minutes. Slice each slab into one–rib bone portions and serve with additional barbecue sauce for dipping. Discard foil and any leftover juices.

Makes 2 slabs

2 whole slabs pork baby back ribs (about 4½ pounds)

Get 'Em Girl Essential Barbecue Rub (page 35)

2 cups Jeniece's Barbecue Sauce (recipe follows)

Jeniece's Barbecue Sauce

1 tablespoon extra virgin olive oil

1 small red onion, finely chopped

¼ teaspoon salt

1 clove garlic, minced

1¼ cups ketchup

2 tablespoons light brown sugar

2 tablespoons yellow mustard

2 tablespoons Worcestershire sauce

2 tablespoons cider vinegar

1 tablespoon hot pepper sauce

1 tablespoon fresh lemon juice

⅛ teaspoon cayenne pepper

¼ teaspoon ground black pepper

*t*he story behind my barbecue sauce is so funny—it dates back to 1987 and my ten-year-old mind thinking I could change the world with ketchup, spices, and a little bit of luck. Turns out that I didn't make a miracle cure, but I did happen to stumble upon a damn good barbecue sauce recipe! —*Jeniece*

1 In a medium saucepan, heat the olive oil over medium heat. Add the onion and cook, stirring occasionally, for 1 minute. Season with salt. Add the garlic and cook, stirring frequently, until the garlic is fragrant, about 1 minute. Stir in the remaining ingredients and bring to a simmer. Reduce the heat to low. Cook, stirring often, until thickened, about 15 minutes.

2 Remove from the heat and use immediately or allow to cool completely and store in an airtight jar in the refrigerator for up to 5 days.

Makes about 2 cups

Bacon and Cheddar–Stuffed Burgers

*W*hether cooked outside over hot coals or on an indoor grill, the result is still the same . . . these burgers are juicy, perfectly seasoned, and full of flavor.

1 Spray a grill with nonstick cooking spray and preheat to medium.

2 Combine the cheese and bacon in a small bowl. In a large bowl, combine the ground beef, onion soup mix, Essential Seasoning, pepper, and water, and mix just until combined. Shape into eight thin patties.

3 Top four patties with ¼ cup of the cheese and bacon mixture each and cover with the remaining patties. Press around the edges of each burger to seal.

4 Place on the grill. Cook for 6 to 8 minutes per side for medium well or until your desired doneness, and serve with your choice of condiments.

Makes 4 servings

1 cup shredded cheddar cheese

8 slices bacon, cooked crisp, drained, and crumbled

1½ pounds lean ground beef or turkey

One 4-serving packet onion soup mix

½ teaspoon Get 'Em Girl Essential Seasoning (page 16)

½ teaspoon ground black pepper

2 tablespoons water

Condiments of your choice

Grilled Marinated Chicken

One 2½- to 3-pound chicken, quartered

1 cup fresh lemon juice (about 5 lemons)

16 ounces bottled Italian salad dressing

1 clove garlic, minced

½ teaspoon salt

½ teaspoon dry mustard

1 Clean and rinse the chicken under cold running water and place in a large bowl. Pour the lemon juice over the chicken; let sit for 1 minute. Rinse well with cold water and pat dry with paper towels. Place the chicken in a resealable plastic bag. Whisk together the Italian dressing, garlic, salt, and dry mustard until thoroughly combined. Pour the marinade over the chicken and seal the bag. Marinate in the refrigerator for at least 4 hours.

2 When ready to cook, preheat the grill to high heat and lightly grease the racks with vegetable oil. Use tongs to take the chicken out of the marinade; discard the remaining marinade. Place the chicken on the grill, bone side down. Grill until the chicken reaches an internal temperature of 190°F on an instant-read thermometer and the juices run clear when pierced with a fork, about 25 minutes per side.

Makes 4 to 6 servings

Uncle Larry's Fried Whiting

*M*y uncle Larry doesn't travel to any family functions without his huge cast-iron pot, which usually hangs in the backyard of his North Carolina home. This is for good reason: because it is a must that anytime we all get together he knows that his fried whiting is the number one requested dish of the weekend. —*Jeniece*

1 Heat about 3 inches of oil in a large pot, preferably cast iron, to 350°F.

2 Meanwhile, rinse the fish fillets and pat them dry with paper towels. Combine the cornmeal, seafood seasoning, and pepper in a large brown paper bag or bowl. In a separate bowl, whisk together the egg and milk until combined well. Coat the fish in the egg mixture, letting the excess drip off. Drop in the cornmeal mixture and shake to coat lightly. Remove one piece at a time, using tongs.

3 Carefully add the fish to the vegetable oil in batches and fry until golden brown, about 8 minutes. Remove and place on a paper towel–lined platter to drain excess grease. Serve immediately.

Makes 6 servings

Vegetable oil, for deep frying

2 pounds whiting fillets

3 cups yellow cornmeal

1 tablespoon seafood seasoning (recommended: Old Bay)

1 teaspoon ground black pepper

1 large egg

½ cup whole milk

Jeniece's Baked Beans

4 slices bacon

1 pound ground pork

1 small onion, chopped

Salt and ground black pepper

One 28-ounce can baked beans, drained

3 tablespoons ketchup

2 tablespoons yellow mustard

¼ cup maple syrup

2 tablespoons light brown sugar

*t*hese aren't your mother's baked beans—in fact, they are more like a main course instead of just a side!

1 Preheat the oven to 350°F.

2 In a large skillet, cook the bacon over medium-low heat until crisp. Place on a paper towel–lined platter, reserving the bacon drippings. Turn the heat up to medium-high, add the ground pork and onions to the drippings, and season with salt and pepper. Cook, breaking up the meat with the back of a wooden spoon, until the meat is no longer pink.

3 Stir in the beans, ketchup, mustard, maple syrup, and sugar. Crumble the bacon and stir into the bean mixture. Transfer the beans to an 8-inch casserole and place in the oven.

4 Bake until the casserole begins to bubble slightly around the edges, about 25 minutes. Allow to cool slightly before serving.

Makes 6 to 8 servings

Crystal's Macaroni Salad

*a*lthough my sister can cook very well, she's more of a "I'll bring the drinks"–type of person, so when she does prepare a dish, she knows she has to come correct—and she definitely came correct with this one. —*Jeniece*

1 Bring a large pot of lightly salted water to a boil over high heat. Add the macaroni and cook according to the package directions for al dente. Drain and rinse under cold water and place in a large bowl.

2 Add the eggs, onions, tuna, relish, mayonnaise, mustard, vinegar, Essential Seasoning, pepper, and onion powder, and stir to combine well. Fold in the tomatoes. Cover with plastic wrap and refrigerate for several hours before serving.

Makes 6 to 8 servings

One 16-ounce package elbow macaroni

4 hard-cooked eggs, chopped

1 small sweet onion, minced

One 6-ounce can solid white tuna packed in water, drained

¼ cup sweet pickle relish

1½ cups mayonnaise

2 tablespoons yellow mustard

1 teaspoon distilled white vinegar

2 teaspoons Get 'Em Girl Essential Seasoning (page 16)

1 teaspoon ground black pepper

¼ teaspoon onion powder

1 small tomato, chopped

Dirty, Dirty Rice

1 tablespoon extra virgin olive oil

1 pound chicken livers, trimmed and finely chopped

12-ounce package sausage

1 small onion, finely chopped

¼ cup finely chopped celery (about 1 stalk)

½ cup finely chopped green bell pepper

1 clove garlic, minced

4 cups hot cooked rice (from 2 cups uncooked)

1 teaspoon salt

½ teaspoon ground black pepper

2 tablespoons chopped fresh parsley

2 scallions, chopped

*t*his Cajun specialty is always a welcome addition to any family gathering table!

1 Heat the olive oil in a large skillet over medium heat. Add the chicken livers and sausage to the skillet and cook, breaking up the sausage with the back of a wooden spoon, until browned (about 10 minutes).

2 Add the onions, celery, green pepper, and garlic to the skillet and cook, stirring occasionally, until the vegetables are tender, about 7 minutes. Stir in the rice, salt, and black pepper. Transfer to a platter and garnish with the parsley and scallions.

Makes 6 to 8 servings

Devilish Eggs

Cut the eggs into halves, lengthwise; remove the yolks and place in a small bowl. Using a fork, mash the yolks well and stir in the mayonnaise, lemon juice, relish, mustard, salt, pepper, and sugar until blended well. Spoon the yolk mixture into the egg whites and sprinkle with paprika. Serve immediately or cover and refrigerate.

Makes 14 pieces

7 hard-cooked eggs

¼ cup mayonnaise

1 teaspoon fresh lemon juice

1 tablespoon sweet pickle relish

1 teaspoon yellow mustard

¼ teaspoon salt

⅛ teaspoon ground white pepper

Pinch of sugar

Paprika, for garnish

Pomegranate Iced Tea with Simple Syrup

6 orange pekoe tea bags

2 cups boiling water

5½ cups cold water

½ cup grenadine

Juice of 1 lemon

1 Place the tea bags in a large measuring cup. Pour the boiling water over the tea bags. Cover and steep for 15 minutes.

2 Discard the tea bags and pour the tea into a 3-quart pitcher. Stir in the cold water, grenadine, and lemon juice; refrigerate until chilled. Serve with simple syrup for sweetening on the side.

Makes 2½ quarts

2 cups water

2 cups sugar

Simple Syrup

Bring the water and sugar to a boil over medium heat in a small saucepan. When the sugar has completely dissolved, remove from heat. Cool to room temperature. Refrigerate until ready to use.

Makes 2 cups

Strawberry Shortcake Trifle

1 Preheat the oven to 325°F. Grease and flour a 10-inch tube pan.

2 Sift together the flour, baking soda, and salt into a large bowl. Beat the butter and sugar in a large bowl, using an electric mixer on high speed, until light and fluffy, about 3 minutes. Add the eggs, one at a time, mixing well after each addition. Add the sour cream, scraping down the sides of the bowl as needed. Reduce the mixer speed to low and slowly add the flour mixture. Mix just until smooth. Stir in the vanilla and lemon peel. Pour the batter into the prepared tube pan. Bake until the top springs back when pressed lightly, about 1½ hours. Remove from the oven and allow to cool completely on a wire rack.

3 Meanwhile, stir together the strawberries and sugar in a medium bowl and set aside.

4 In a large bowl, beat together the cream cheese and condensed milk. In another large bowl, whip the cream on high with an electric mixer until thickened. Add the confectioners' sugar and vanilla and continue to whip until stiff peaks are formed. Using a silicone spatula, gently fold the whipped cream into the cream cheese mixture until combined.

5 To assemble: Using a serrated knife, slice the pound cake into ½-inch cubes. In a large trifle dish or glass bowl, layer in this order:

> One-third of the cake cubes
> One-third of the macerated strawberries, with the juice
> One-third of the custard

6 Repeat layers two more times, ending with custard. Garnish with whole strawberries.

Makes 8 to 10 servings

SOUR CREAM POUND CAKE

2 cups all-purpose flour

½ teaspoon baking soda

½ teaspoon salt

½ pound (2 sticks) unsalted butter, softened

3 cups granulated sugar

6 large eggs, room temperature

1 cup sour cream

½ teaspoon vanilla extract

1 teaspoon grated lemon peel

MACERATED STRAWBERRIES

2 pints fresh strawberries, hulled and halved (save a few whole for garnish)

¼ cup granulated sugar

CUSTARD

One 8-ounce package cream cheese, softened

One 14-ounce can sweetened condensed milk

2 cups heavy cream

2 tablespoons confectioners' sugar

½ teaspoon vanilla extract

Caribbean Jerk Chicken

One 3-pound chicken, cut into 8 pieces

½ cup lemon juice (about 8 lemons)

½ teaspoon salt

½ teaspoon ground black pepper

½ teaspoon sweet paprika

¼ cup jerk seasoning (recommended: Walkerswood)

2 tablespoons extra virgin olive oil

1 Clean and rinse the chicken under cold running water and place in a large bowl. Pour the lemon juice over the chicken; let sit for 1 minute. Rinse well with cold water and pat dry with paper towels. Season with salt, pepper, and paprika and place in a resealable plastic bag.

2 In a small bowl, mix together the jerk seasoning and olive oil. Pour over the chicken, seal, and allow to marinate, turning occasionally, in the refrigerator for at least 1 hour, preferably overnight.

3 When ready to cook, preheat the oven to 450°F. Remove the chicken from the bag and place in a shallow roasting pan, skin side down. Bake, turning occasionally and basting with pan juices after 15 minutes, then again before browning, about 30 minutes.

4 Turn on the broiler. Broil, skin side up, about 4 inches from the heat, until the skin is brown and crispy, 2 to 3 minutes.

Makes 4 to 6 servings

Spice-Rubbed Grilled Tilapia

1 Place the fish in a shallow baking dish. In a small bowl, whisk together the Essential Barbecue Rub, salt, and olive oil. Pour the spice mixture over the fish and gently rub into the fish. Cover with plastic wrap and marinate in the refrigerator for 1 hour.

2 Meanwhile, preheat an outdoor grill to medium. Brush the grill grates with oil to prevent sticking. Place the fish on the grill. Cook just until the fish flakes when tested with a fork, turning once, about 6 minutes per side. Serve immediately.

Makes 6 servings

TIP

To save time on cleanup and to prevent fish from breaking up, cover grill grates with aluminum foil and poke holes all over with the tines of a fork.

Six 6-ounce tilapia fillets

3 tablespoons Get 'Em Girl Essential Barbecue Rub (page 35)

¼ teaspoon salt

¼ cup extra virgin olive oil, plus more for brushing

Grilled Corn on the Cob with Smoked Bacon Butter

8 ears corn

½ pound (2 sticks) unsalted butter, softened

½ pound smoked bacon, cooked, drained, and crumbled

1½ teaspoons honey

¼ cup chopped chives

Salt and ground black pepper

*O*kay, so this recipe is a bit on the extreme side, but it is so good! If you try this recipe at least once during the summer months, you'll be more than satisfied. You worked out all spring, so save this one until the very last barbecue of the year and you won't feel too bad. *— Joan*

1 Gently pull back the husk, exposing the corn, making sure not to remove the husk. Using a brush, remove the corn silk. Soak the corn in a large bowl of cold water for 30 minutes to prevent the husking from burning. Preheat the grill to medium.

2 Meanwhile, place the butter, bacon, honey, and chives in a medium bowl and beat with an electric mixer on medium speed until thoroughly combined. Season to taste with salt and pepper.

3 Remove the corn from the water and pat dry with a paper towel. Recover each ear of corn with the husk, place on the hot grill, and cover the grill. Grill, turning occasionally, until the corn is tender, 15 to 20 minutes.

4 When ready to serve, carefully pull back the husk and brush the kernels generously with the butter.

Makes 8 servings

Joan's Honey Cornbread

i get a lot of requests to make cornbread at just about every get-together; please be prepared for the same. — *Joan*

1 Preheat the oven to 400°F. Spray an 8-inch square baking dish with nonstick cooking spray.

2 In a large bowl, whisk together the flour, cornmeal, sugar, salt, and baking powder. In a small bowl, combine the eggs, milk, vegetable oil, butter, and honey until well mixed. Slowly stir the egg mixture into the cornmeal mixture just until combined; pour batter into the prepared pan.

3 Bake until a wooden skewer inserted into the center of the cornbread comes out clean, 20 to 25 minutes.

4 Remove from the oven and allow to cool slightly before slicing and serving with additional butter.

Makes 12 servings

1 cup all-purpose flour

1 cup yellow cornmeal

⅔ cup sugar

1 teaspoon salt

1 tablespoon baking powder

2 large eggs

1 cup whole milk

⅓ cup vegetable oil

3 tablespoons unsalted butter, melted

¼ cup honey

Red Bliss–Caesar Potato Salad

4 large Red Bliss potatoes, peeled and diced into ½-inch cubes

½ small red onion, finely chopped

¼ cup finely chopped small green bell pepper

2 hard-cooked eggs, finely chopped

2 teaspoons Get 'Em Girl Essential Seasoning (page 16)

½ teaspoon ground black pepper

¼ teaspoon onion powder

1 teaspoon sugar

1 cup mayonnaise

1 tablespoon yellow mustard

1 tablespoon creamy Caesar salad dressing (recommended: Ken's)

i added a Get 'Em Girl twist to a traditional Southern dish.

—*Joan*

1 Bring a large pot of water to a boil over high heat. Add the potatoes to the boiling water and cook just until fork tender, 8 to 10 minutes; be sure not to overcook. Drain in a colander and place in a large bowl. Add the onions, green peppers, and eggs and mix gently but thoroughly.

2 In a small bowl, mix together the Essential Seasoning, black pepper, onion powder, sugar, mayonnaise, mustard, and Caesar dressing. With a silicone spatula, gently fold the mayonnaise mixture into the potatoes, making sure not to break up the potatoes. Cover and chill for several hours before serving.

Makes 4 to 6 servings

Spiked Fruit Salad

Whisk together the wine, lime juice, sugar, and honey in a small bowl. Place all the fruit in a large serving bowl and pour the lime mixture over the salad. Toss to coat, taste, and adjust to your taste with additional sugar or lime juice. Refrigerate until chilled and ready to serve.

Makes 8 to 10 servings

½ cup sweet dessert wine, chilled

¼ cup fresh lime juice

¼ cup sugar

2 tablespoons honey

1 pineapple, peeled, cored, and cut into 1-inch pieces

1 mango, peeled, pitted, and cut into 1-inch pieces

1 pint strawberries, hulled and quartered

½ pound seedless grapes

½ honeydew melon, seeded and scooped into balls

Spicy Turkey Burgers

1 teaspoon Get 'Em Girl Essential Seasoning (page 16)

¼ teaspoon cayenne pepper

½ teaspoon ground black pepper

1 teaspoon garlic powder

½ teaspoon onion powder

2 large eggs

2 tablespoons chili sauce

2 pounds lean ground turkey

4 to 6 hamburger buns, split and lightly toasted

TOPPINGS

Pepper Jack cheese slices

Lettuce leaves

Tomato slices

Red onion slices

1 Mix together the Essential Seasoning, cayenne, black pepper, garlic powder, onion powder, eggs, and chili sauce in a large bowl. Add the turkey and mix well. Shape into 4 large burgers or 6 small burgers and place on a platter or baking sheet. Refrigerate for 1 hour to allow burgers to set. Meanwhile, preheat a grill to medium.

2 Brush the grill grates with oil to prevent sticking. Place the turkey burgers on the grill and cook until the center in no longer pink, about 8 minutes per side. Serve on a bun with toppings of your choice.

Makes 4 to 6 servings

Hilton's Smoked Ribs

*m*y stepfather loves to grill outdoors. The trick to smoking ribs is to make sure the meat never touches the fire. If you would like to use barbecue sauce, begin basting the ribs with your favorite sauce 15 minutes before removing them from the grill. —*Shakara*

1½ pounds ribs, washed and trimmed of fat

¾ cup distilled white vinegar

¼ cup water

Prepare the grill for indirect grilling (place coals on sides of the grill only) and preheat to medium. Place the ribs on the side of the grill not directly over the heat and close the lid. Combine vinegar and water in a bowl and smoke the ribs, basting occasionally with the vinegar mixture, until the ribs are tender and fully cooked, about 4 hours.

Makes 4 servings

TAKE NOTE

The ribs may have a pink ring around them; this is an indication of a long smoking process and not undercooked meat.

TIP

To prepare the grill for indirect grilling, place the coals at the far ends of the grill if using a charcoal grill, leaving the center of the grill free of coals. Place foil in the center to act as a drip pan. Light your coals as usual and place the food in the center of the grill. For a gas grill, only turn on one side of the grill for a two-burner grill or two for a three-burner, cooking the food on the burner that is unlit.

Honey Barbecue Chicken Quarters

2 pounds chicken quarters, mixed

Juice of 1 lemon

2 tablespoons Get 'Em Girl
Essential Barbecue Rub (page 35)

2 cups hickory wood chips, soaked
in water for 30 minutes

2 cups Simple Honey Barbecue
Sauce, for serving (page 67)

1 Clean and rinse chicken under cold running water and place in a large bowl. Add the lemon juice and let sit for 1 minute. Rinse well with cold water and pat dry with paper towels. Rub the Essential Barbecue Rub all over the chicken and under the skin and let sit while you prepare the grill.

2 Prepare the grill for indirect grilling (see page 93) and preheat to medium. If using a charcoal grill, scatter the wood chips over the coals; if using a gas grill, place the wood chips in a smoker pouch and place on the grill, leaving enough room for the chicken.

3 Place the chicken on the side of the grill not directly over the heat, cover, and cook until the chicken reaches an internal temperature of 180°F on an instant-read thermometer, 25 to 30 minutes per side. Remove the chicken from the grill and transfer to a serving plate. Serve with the Honey Barbecue Sauce on the side.

Makes 4 to 6 servings

Barbecue Shrimp Skewers

1 In a large bowl, whisk together all the ingredients except the shrimp. Add the shrimp to the spice mixture and toss to coat. Cover and let sit in refrigerator.

2 Preheat grill to medium. Brush grill grates with oil to prevent sticking. Thread the shrimp onto the skewers and place on the grill. Cook until the shrimp are pink and have light grill marks, making sure not to over-cook, about 3 minutes per side. Remove and serve immediately.

Makes 4 to 6 servings

¼ cup vegetable oil

1 tablespoon minced garlic

¼ teaspoon dried thyme

1½ teaspoons paprika

½ teaspoon chili powder

1½ teaspoons salt

1 teaspoon ground cumin

1 tablespoon light brown sugar

½ teaspoon ground black pepper

¼ teaspoon dried oregano

¼ teaspoon cayenne pepper

½ teaspoon onion powder

1 tablespoon fresh chopped cilantro

Juice of 1 lemon

2 pounds large shrimp, peeled and deveined

Four to six 7-inch bamboo skewers, soaked in water until ready to use

Sandra's Pasta and Seafood Salad

8 ounces packaged elbow macaroni

2 stalks celery, finely chopped

½ teaspoon celery seed

½ small onion, finely chopped

½ teaspoon onion powder

¼ teaspoon garlic powder

½ teaspoon yellow mustard

3 tablespoons sweet pickle relish

One 6-ounce can solid white tuna packed in water, drained

½ pound lump crabmeat

Salt and ground black pepper

¾ cup mayonnaise

i love my momma's cooking! Her pasta and seafood salad is a staple during our summer cookouts! — *Shakara*

Bring a large pot of lightly salted water to a boil over high heat. Add the macaroni and cook according to the package directions for al dente. Drain in a colander, rinse under cold water, and drain again. Place in a large bowl. Add the celery, celery seed, onions, onion powder, garlic powder, mustard, relish, tuna, crabmeat, salt and pepper, and mayonnaise, and stir to combine well. Cover with plastic wrap and refrigerate for several hours before serving.

Makes 4 to 6 servings

Strawberry Pudding

1 Heat the strawberries, sugar, and gelatin in a medium saucepan, stirring constantly, until gelatin is dissolved. Set aside and let cool.

2 In a medium bowl, whisk together the vanilla pudding and milk until thickened. Stir in the sour cream. With a silicone spatula, fold in one container of whipped topping.

3 In a 9 by 13-inch baking dish, layer wafers, pudding, and strawberry topping. Repeat until all are used. Top with the second container of whipped topping. Garnish with sliced strawberries and refrigerate.

Makes 8 to 10 servings

2 pints strawberries, hulled and sliced (save some for garnish)

½ cup sugar

One 3-ounce package strawberry gelatin

Two 3.4-ounce packages vanilla instant pudding

3 cups cold milk

1 cup sour cream

Two 8-ounce containers frozen whipped topping, thawed

2⅔ packages (12 ounces each) vanilla wafers

Frances B's Punch

5 packs lemon-lime unsweetened
soft drink mix powder
(recommended: Kool-Aid)

2 quarts of water

One 46-ounce can pineapple juice

5 cups sugar

*m*y cousin Frances Bryant makes the best punch. I called her house for weeks trying to get the recipe. Imagine my surprise when I found out it was just Kool-Aid and pineapple juice. — *Shakara*

In a large pitcher, combine drink mix, pineapple juice, and sugar, stirring continuously to dissolve sugar. Serve chilled.

Makes about 7½ quarts

Let's Have a Shower!

Welcome Baby Shower, Tea Party

Lump Crab Tea Sandwiches

Warm Vanilla Tea Cakes

Brown Sugar Scones with Praline Butter

The Perfect Pot of Tea

Always the Bridesmaid . . . Bridal Shower

Soy-Marinated Pork Tenderloin

Mixed Green Salad with Candied Pecans and Bacon Vinaigrette

Roasted Garlic and Sun-Dried Tomato Crostini

Herb Blinis with Pecan Granny Smith Apple Slaw

Cucumber Mint Tea Sandwiches

Like Sunshine Lemon Cupcakes

*i*t's almost time! Your best girlfriend is a month or so away from one of the most amazing days in her life, and as much as it is a blessing, she just cannot wait to give birth. Her feet are swollen, her back aches, and she feels like she's birthing David Beckham with all the kicking going on. Nothing would make this expectant mom happier than an afternoon tea party with great friends, much-needed baby essentials, and delicious treats.

I still remember the first shower I hosted as if it were yesterday, I was so excited! My best friend Amithy was pregnant with my goddaughter Shanya, she was recently married, and she'd just graduated from college, so I wanted the shower to celebrate the baby as well as all of the other new and exciting things going on in her life. I will never forget, it had to be the hottest day of the summer and I tried to cram over a hundred people in my mother's living room. Her "little air conditioner that could" was working overtime and everyone in attendance was sweating buckets. Although grateful, Amithy clearly couldn't wait for the event to come to an end—and once over, I realized that the "shower" that I worked so hard to put together was much more about the hostess than the guest of honor. She would have appreciated ten of her closest friends getting together for an afternoon picnic in the park to celebrate the new arrival—wish I had known then! —*Jeniece*

I've been a bridesmaid in at least seven weddings and I've had the honor of hosting several bridal showers. One of my most memorable showers occurred when my two good friends Charles and Nicole got engaged. They were best friends for well over ten years and inseparable; so what better way to celebrate the festive occasion but with a surprise Jack & Jill Shower! The idea sounded really great, but the thought of having to decorate, accommodate, entertain and feed a hundred people was frightening. However, with extensive planning and organization, everything went well. Here is a bridal shower checklist that I use to help keep me organized and sane! —*Joan*

Three Months Before

1 Talk to the bride about what type of shower she wants. Does she want a tea party? Jack & Jill? Friday night soiree?
2 Meet with other bridesmaids to brainstorm ideas, set a date, and create a budget and menu.
3 Make a to-do list, then divide and conquer with everyone who has agreed to help.
4 Make a list of possible locations; call and check for availability.
5 Create a guest list.
6 Mail or e-mail out-of-town guests a "save the date" note.

Two Months Before

1 Confirm reservation for location as soon as possible.
2 Order invitations or purchase materials needed to create invitations.
3 Order special menu items from caterer/baker, coffee urns, and other equipment from a rental company, if necessary.
4 Meet with bridesmaids again to finalize decisions about decorations, music, favors, games, and table linens.

One Month Before

1　Mail invitations, and include information about the couple's registries.
2　Order flower arrangements.
3　Purchase favors, paper goods, and decorations.
4　Purchase spirits for cocktails.

Two Weeks Before

1　Buy shower gift for bride.
2　Make shopping list for food and any hard-to-find ingredients.
3　Pick up everything people have graciously offered to let you borrow for the shower.
4　Conduct final RSVP headcount.

One Week Before

1　Confirm deliveries (add additional tables or chairs if needed).
2　Confirm reservations.
3　Prepare shower games and activities.
4　Assemble and gift-wrap prizes for game winners.

One Day Before

1　Prepare menu items that can be made in advance or at least complete prep work.
2　Set up tables, chairs and decorate.
3　Confirm with bridesmaids and finalize who's bringing what; ask them to arrive early to assist with any final tasks.
4　Complete any last-minute errands.

Day Of

1　Cook and prepare food and cocktails.
2　Receive and display flowers.
3　Set out the food.
4　Exhale, grab a cocktail, and enjoy your best friend's day.

Lump Crab Tea Sandwiches

1 In a small bowl, combine the cream cheese and chives. Spread the mixture onto one side of each slice of bread. In a separate bowl, combine the crab meat, mayonnaise, lemon juice, salt, and pepper, and mix to combine well.

2 Lay out 10 slices of bread and spread about ¼ cup of the crab mixture onto each slice. Top with the remaining bread slices. Trim the crusts off all of the sandwiches and slice each sandwich crosswise into four triangles.

Makes 40 tea sandwiches

¾ **cup cream cheese, softened**

¼ **cup finely chopped chives**

20 slices sturdy white bread

2 cups finely chopped lump crabmeat

½ **cup mayonnaise**

1 tablespoon fresh lemon juice

1 teaspoon salt

½ **teaspoon ground black pepper**

Warm Vanilla Tea Cakes

1½ cups sugar

10⅔ tablespoons (1⅓ sticks)
softened, unsalted butter

2 large eggs

2 teaspoons vanilla extract

2 cups all-purpose flour

1 Preheat the oven to 400°F.

2 Beat together 1 cup sugar and the butter in a large bowl with an electric mixer on high speed for about 2 minutes, until the mixture is light and fluffy. Beat in the eggs one at a time, then the vanilla, scraping down the sides of the bowl as necessary.

3 Reduce the mixer speed to low and gradually add the flour until combined well. Drop by the tablespoonful about 1 inch apart onto an ungreased baking sheet.

4 Place the remaining ½ cup sugar in a shallow dish. Dip the bottom of a glass in the sugar and flatten out the dough. Bake until the cakes are golden, about 7 to 10 minutes. Remove and cool slightly on a wire rack before serving.

Makes about 3 dozen cakes

Brown Sugar Scones with Praline Butter

*Y*ou will be considered "the hostess with the mostess" when you serve these delicious scones.

1 Preheat the oven to 400°F. Line a baking sheet with parchment paper.

2 Mix together the flour, sugar, baking powder, baking soda, and salt into a large bowl. Using a fork, blend the butter into the flour mixture until the largest pieces are the size of small peas. Whisk together the milk and the maple syrup in a small bowl. Make a well in the center of the flour mixture and pour in the milk mixture; stir just until the dough comes together.

3 Turn the dough out onto a lightly floured work surface and with floured hands gently fold the dough over itself 10 times and pat it out to ¾-inch thickness. Cut the dough into 3-inch squares using a knife, then cut each square in half to form triangles. Place on the prepared baking sheet. Brush the top of each scone with additional milk and sprinkle with brown sugar. Bake until the tops are golden brown, about 20 minutes.

4 Cool on a wire rack and serve with Praline Butter.

Makes 8 scones

2½ cups all-purpose flour, plus more for shaping

¼ cup light brown sugar, plus more for sprinkling

1½ teaspoons baking powder

½ teaspoon baking soda

½ teaspoon salt

8 tablespoons (1 stick) unsalted butter, chilled

¾ cup whole milk, plus more for brushing

½ cup maple syrup

Praline Butter (recipe follows), for serving

¼ cup sugar

½ cup chopped pecans

9 tablespoons (1⅛ sticks) unsalted butter

½ teaspoon vanilla extract

Praline Butter

1 Line a baking sheet with parchment paper.

2 Pour the sugar into a medium heavy-bottomed skillet and cook over medium heat, stirring often, until the sugar begins to melt. Carefully add the pecans and 1 tablespoon butter to the sugar. Reduce the heat to low. Cook, stirring constantly, until the sugar has completely melted and has turned a medium amber.

3 Remove the skillet from the heat and spread nuts onto the prepared baking sheet, using a silicone spatula. Allow the pecans to cool completely before breaking into small pieces. Place the pecans into a resealable plastic bag and crush with a rolling pin.

4 In a small bowl, mix the remaining butter, vanilla, and nuts. Serve immediately or cover with plastic wrap and refrigerate for later use. Let the praline butter stand out at room temperature to soften before serving.

Makes about 1 cup

The Perfect Pot of Tea

1 Fill a tea kettle with cold water and set it to boil. As the water nears a boil, pour a little of it into the teapot you plan to serve your tea in to warm it, swirling the water around and then discarding it.

2 Place the tea leaves into the empty teapot. Pour the boiling water into the teapot and let the tea steep for 3 to 6 minutes. Gently stir before pouring the tea through a strainer into teacups.

3 Serve immediately with lemon slices or milk and honey or sugar cubes.

Makes 4 cups

1 quart cold water

4 teaspoons loose breakfast tea leaves

Lemon slices

Honey

Milk

Sugar cubes

Soy-Marinated Pork Tenderloin

¼ cup soy sauce

¾ cup hoisin sauce

¾ cup dry sherry

¼ cup rice wine vinegar

2 cloves garlic, minced

2 pounds pork tenderloin

2 tablespoons extra virgin olive oil

1 In a large bowl, mix together the soy sauce, hoisin sauce, sherry, rice wine vinegar, and garlic. Place the tenderloin in the bowl, turn to coat with the marinade, and cover tightly. Marinate in the refrigerator for 4 hours.

2 When ready to cook, preheat the oven to 400°F. Heat the olive oil in a large skillet over medium-high heat. Put the tenderloin in the pan and cook, turning occasionally, until all sides are browned, about 10 minutes. Transfer meat to a roasting pan and roast for 20 minutes. Slice against the grain on a diagonal and serve.

Makes 6 to 8 servings

Mixed Green Salad with Candied Pecans and Bacon Vinaigrette

1 Preheat the oven to 350°F. Line two baking sheets with parchment paper.

2 Spread the pecans in a single layer on one of the baking sheets and bake until lightly toasted, about 6 minutes. Remove and set aside to cool completely.

3 Pour the sugar into a heavy-bottomed medium saucepan and cook over medium heat, stirring often with a wooden spoon, until the sugar is melted and has turned a medium amber (about 7 minutes). Quickly stir in the pecans, making sure to coat each piece with sugar.

4 With a wooden spoon, carefully spread the pecans out on the second baking sheet (the nuts will be extremely hot) and carefully break apart the clusters with a fork. Sprinkle the candied nuts with salt and allow them to cool completely before using.

5 Wash the mixed greens thoroughly and dry in a salad spinner. Transfer to a salad bowl, cover with damp paper towels, and refrigerate.

6 In a jar with a tight-fitting lid, combine the olive oil, vinegar, bacon drippings, brown sugar, mustard, salt, and pepper, and shake vigorously until slightly thickened and combined well. Let sit until ready to serve.

7 Pour the vinaigrette over the mixed greens and top with the candied pecans. Toss to coat leaves thoroughly. Serve immediately.

Makes 4 to 6 servings

CANDIED PECANS

1½ cups pecan halves

½ cup sugar

Pinch of salt

One 9-ounce bag mixed greens

¼ cup extra virgin olive oil

¼ cup cider vinegar

2 tablespoons bacon drippings

1 tablespoon light brown sugar

1 tablespoon whole-grain mustard

½ teaspoon salt

¼ teaspoon ground black pepper

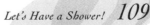

Roasted Garlic and Sun-Dried Tomato Crostini

2 heads roasted garlic (recipe follows)

One 8-ounce package cream cheese, softened

½ cup crumbled feta cheese

1 teaspoon dried oregano

½ cup drained sun-dried tomatoes (packed in oil)

1 small loaf ciabatta bread, cut into ½-inch slices

1 In a medium bowl, beat the garlic with the cheeses and oregano until smooth. Finely chop the tomatoes and add to the cheese mixture. Stir until well combined. Cover and refrigerate 6 to 8 hours to blend flavors.

2 Preheat the broiler to medium. Place the bread on the broiler rack and cook until golden and crispy, about 2 minutes. Watch carefully so that it doesn't burn.

3 Arrange the toasts on a serving dish. Top each slice with a spoonful of the tomato mixture and serve immediately.

Makes 4 to 6 servings

---

2 large heads of garlic

2 tablespoons extra virgin olive oil

Pinch of salt and ground black pepper

Roasted Garlic

Preheat the oven to 400°F. Cut off ¼ inch of the top of the garlic heads to expose the cloves. Place garlic heads in aluminum foil, drizzle with oil, and season with salt and pepper. Cover tightly with foil and bake until skins are golden and the cloves are tender, about 45 minutes to 1 hour. Cool and squeeze garlic cloves from skins.

Herb Blinis with
Pecan Granny Smith Apple Slaw

1 In a medium bowl, combine all the slaw ingredients, coating the apples evenly. Set aside.

2 In a separate medium bowl, combine flour, buttermilk, egg, herbs, shallots, butter, baking powder, and baking soda until well blended.

3 Spray a nonstick skillet with nonstick spray and heat over medium heat. Working in batches, drop batter by heaping tablespoonfuls into skillet, spreading each pancake to a 3-inch round with back of spoon. Cook until bottom is golden, about 2 minutes. Turn over and cook until second side is golden, about another minute. Transfer to a paper towel–lined plate and cover loosely with aluminum foil to keep warm. Continue working in batches until you have finished your batter, spraying the skillet with nonstick cooking spray at the beginning of each batch.

4 To assemble: Lay the blinis on a plate and top each one with about 2 teaspoons of the slaw, a pecan half, and serve.

Makes about 16 blinis

SLAW

½ Granny Smith apple, cored and cut into ⅛-inch-thick, 1-inch-long matchsticks

1 tablespoon fresh lemon juice

¼ cup pecan halves, lightly toasted

1 tablespoon honey

2 teaspoons salt

1 teaspoon ground black pepper

1 tablespoon chopped fresh chives

2 tablespoons extra virgin olive oil

BLINIS

¾ cup all-purpose flour

¾ cup buttermilk

1 large egg, beaten

¼ cup chopped fresh herbs (parsley, chives, tarragon, mint, or whatever you like)

2 tablespoons chopped shallots

2 tablespoons unsalted butter, melted

¾ teaspoon baking powder

¼ teaspoon baking soda

16 pecan halves

Cucumber Mint Tea Sandwiches

1 large seedless cucumber (English)

8 ounces mascarpone cheese

2 ounces mayonnaise

2 tablespoons finely chopped fresh mint, plus more for garnish

Juice and grated peel of 1 lemon

1 teaspoon salt

1 teaspoon ground black pepper

8 slices sourdough bread (or any thick, fairly dense bread you like)

1 With a very sharp knife or a mandolin, slice the cucumber into disks ⅛ inch thick. Dry the slices in single layers between paper towels to ensure there isn't any excess moisture, and leave between the paper towels until you are ready to assemble.

2 In a medium bowl, combine the mascarpone, mayonnaise, mint, lemon juice and peel, salt, and pepper, and blend until all the ingredients are combined to a smooth spread.

3 To assemble: Take one slice of bread and spread about 1 tablespoon of mint spread in an even layer. Arrange a single layer of cucumbers atop the spread, overlapping each one slightly. Spread a second slice of bread with another tablespoon of the spread, laying the spread side down atop the cucumber layer. Spread another tablespoon of the spread on the exposed side of the bread, then arrange another slightly overlapped layer of cucumbers on top. Repeat the process with the rest of the bread, giving you two open-faced layered sandwiches.

4 With a very sharp knife, cut the crust of each sandwich evenly, leaving you with perfect squares, and cut each squared sandwich into four pieces. Garnish with some mint leaves on top and serve.

Makes about 16 sandwiches

Like Sunshine Lemon Cupcakes

*W*e get so many requests for these cupcakes that we decided to place them in the book. The flavor is so bright that they will literally wake you up.

1 Preheat the oven to 350°F. Place paper cupcake liners into two 12-cup muffin pans.

2 Beat the butter and sugar in a large bowl with an electric mixer on medium until light and fluffy, about 5 minutes. Add the eggs, one at a time, and the lemon peel.

3 Sift together the flour, baking powder, baking soda, and salt into a separate bowl. Combine the lemon juice, sour cream, and vanilla in a small bowl. Slowly add the flour and sour cream alternately to the batter, beginning and ending with flour.

4 Using a ¼-cup measuring cup, pour the batter into the prepared muffin pans. Bake until a toothpick inserted into the center of the cupcakes comes out clean, about 15 to 18 minutes. Remove from the oven and allow to cool completely in the pans.

5 Meanwhile, heat the sugar and lemon juice in a small saucepan just until the sugar is dissolved. Spoon the lemon syrup over the cooled cupcakes and refrigerate until ready to serve.

Makes 24 cupcakes

½ pound (2 sticks) unsalted butter, softened

2 cups sugar

4 large eggs

Grated peel of 3 lemons

3 cups unbleached all-purpose flour

½ teaspoon baking powder

½ teaspoon baking soda

1 teaspoon salt

¼ cup fresh lemon juice

1 cup sour cream

1 teaspoon vanilla extract

LEMON SYRUP

1 cup sugar

⅔ cup fresh lemon juice

Meet the Family
Sunday Brunch

She's the One
Easy Buttermilk Pancakes
Simple Corned Beef Hash
Overnight Sausage and Cheese Strata
Honey Banana Crunch Yogurt Parfait
Aunt Melody's Bloody Mary (page 203)

Meet Prince Charming
Sweet Potato Waffles with Honey Butter
Baked Cheese Grits
Easy Coffee Cake Muffins

Perfect Combination
Maple Pecan Crumble French Toast Casserole
Scrambled Eggs with Butter and Chives
Hilton's Hash Browns
Bangin' Buttermilk Biscuits
Cream Scones
Cranberry Punch (page 204)

*t*his is the fourth Sunday you've missed 11:00 a.m. service and your mother called to inquire about the man who has been beating Jesus' time—to which you quickly interject that the two of you have been going to 7:00 a.m. service at his church (nice save!). In actuality, the two of you have been practically living in the same space for six months and have barely come up for air—you both decide that now might be the right time to meet each other's family.

The family could be just his or her parents, or it can get as deep as the children, parents, grandparents, cousins—to which we might say slow down! No matter whom you want to introduce your lover to, it's best done over great food and good company. So instead of making reservations, might we suggest the both of you rolling up your sleeves and putting your hands to work to create a delicious *after-service* Sunday brunch that will satisfy the pickiest palate? Okay, let's get started.

(from bottom right, clockwise): Grilled PB&J Cut-Out Sandwiches, DIY Yellow Cupcakes with Easy Buttercream Frosting, and Chicken Fingers

(from bottom right, clockwise): Sassy Girl Sliders,
Pears and Blue Cheese on Endive Spears, and Crispy Baked Potato Wedges

(from bottom right, clockwise): Sandra's Pasta and Seafood Salad, Grilled Corn on the Cob with Smoked Bacon Butter, Honey Barbecue Chicken Quarters, Strawberry Shortcake Trifle, Pomegranate Iced Tea, and Joan's Honey Cornbread

(from left, clockwise): Kettle-Cooked Homemade Potato Chips, Red Velvet Sandwich Cakes, Sparkling Lemonade, Picnic Potato Salad, and Curried Chicken Salad on Ciabatta

(from bottom, clockwise): Spinach and Roasted Pear Salad with Pomegranate Vinaigrette, Vegetable Rigatoni Bolognese, and Parmesan Crisps

(from left, clockwise): Poppin' Black Cherry Martini, Lip Puckering Strawberry Lemonade, Cocoa Cure Chocolate Martini, and Cheryl's Deluxe Frozen Margarita

(from bottom, clockwise): Roasted Garlic and Sun-Dried Tomato Crostini,
Like Sunshine Lemon Cupcakes, Cucumber Mint Tea Sandwiches,
and Herb Blinis with Pecan Granny Smith Apple Slaw

Easy Buttermilk Pancakes

*t*hese pancakes are the little black dress of breakfast! Enjoy simply with maple syrup or topped with your favorite fresh fruits and berries.

1 Sift together the flour, sugar, baking powder, baking soda, and salt into a large bowl. In a separate bowl, whisk together the buttermilk, milk, eggs, and melted butter. Combine the flour and buttermilk mixtures and stir just until combined; lumps in the batter are fine. Do not overmix.

2 Spray a griddle or large skillet with nonstick cooking spray before each batch of pancakes and heat over medium heat. Spoon ½ cup of batter onto the griddle for each pancake. Flip when bubbles begin to appear on top of the pancakes, about 2 to 3 minutes. Cook the second side about 1 minute and serve with additional butter and maple syrup.

Makes 8 pancakes

2 cups all-purpose flour

3 tablespoons sugar

2 teaspoons baking powder

½ teaspoon baking soda

½ teaspoon salt

2 cups buttermilk

⅓ cup whole milk

2 large eggs

4 tablespoons (½ stick) unsalted butter, melted

Butter, for serving

Maple syrup, for serving

Simple Corned Beef Hash

6 tablespoons (¾ stick) unsalted butter

3 tablespoons extra virgin olive oil

5 medium Russet potatoes, peeled and diced into ¼-inch cubes

1 large onion, minced

Two 12-ounce cans corned beef or 4 cups finely chopped cooked corned beef

1½ cups reduced-sodium beef broth

Salt and ground black pepper

Fresh chopped parsley, for garnish

*t*his is an absolute must when we've been partying and hit our favorite diner! Add a fried egg and toast and you've got good eats!

1 Melt the butter and olive oil together in a large skillet over medium heat. Add the potatoes and onions and cook, stirring occasionally, until the onions are tender, about 5 minutes.

2 Break up the canned corned beef into chunks, if using. Stir the corned beef into the potato and onion mixture. Add the beef broth, reduce the heat to low, and cover. Simmer for about 10 minutes until the potatoes are tender and the broth has almost completely reduced. Season to taste with salt and pepper, transfer to a serving dish, and garnish with parsley.

Makes 6 to 8 servings

Overnight Sausage and Cheese Strata

*t*his delicious cheese strata should be prepared the night before, unless your brunch is more like supper.

1 In a large skillet, cook the sausage over medium-high heat, stirring, until no longer pink, about 10 minutes. Remove the sausage from the skillet with a slotted spoon, leaving the drippings in the pan, and place in a large bowl.

2 Add the onions and potatoes to the drippings. Cook, stirring occasionally, for about 5 minutes until the onions are translucent. Using a slotted spoon, add the potato mixture to the sausage and mix gently, being careful not to break up the potatoes.

3 Generously grease a 9 by 13-inch baking dish. Layer half of the bread cubes over the bottom of the dish. Cover with all of the sausage mixture and ½ cup of the cheese. Top with the remaining bread cubes and sprinkle with the remaining cheese.

4 In a medium bowl, whisk together the eggs, milk, mustard, and salt and pepper until well blended. Slowly and evenly pour the egg mixture over the bread cubes and gently press down with a metal spatula. Cover with plastic wrap and refrigerate overnight.

5 When ready to bake: Preheat the oven to 350°F and remove the strata from the refrigerator, remove the plastic wrap, and allow it to come to room temperature, about 20 minutes. Bake, uncovered, until a knife inserted into the center of the strata comes out clean, 50 to 60 minutes.

Makes 6 to 8 servings

1½ pounds bulk breakfast sausage

1 small onion, chopped

2 large Russet potatoes, peeled and cubed

6 slices white sandwich bread, cubed

3 cups shredded cheddar cheese

7 large eggs

2½ cups whole milk

1 teaspoon yellow mustard

Salt and ground black pepper

Honey Banana Crunch Yogurt Parfait

One 6-ounce cup plain or vanilla yogurt

1 ripe banana, sliced

¼ cup granola, plus more for garnish

¼ cup honey

a healthy and delicious breakfast option that kids and adults will both enjoy.

In a parfait glass, layer one-third of the yogurt, 4 to 5 banana slices, 2 tablespoons of granola, and drizzle with 2 tablespoons of honey. Repeat the layering once more and top with remaining yogurt. Garnish with granola and serve or refrigerate immediately.

Makes 1 serving

MAKE IT YOUR OWN

Use any fruits or berries that you enjoy, substitute chopped nuts for the granola, or change the flavor of the yogurt to make it all yours!

Sweet Potato Waffles with Honey Butter

1 Preheat the waffle iron.

2 Pierce the sweet potatoes all over with a fork and place on a paper towel–lined microwave-safe dish, about 1 inch apart. Microwave on high power for 6 to 8 minutes, turning over halfway through. Remove and allow to cool slightly. Once cool enough to handle, peel and mash the potatoes in a small bowl.

3 In a medium bowl, whisk together the milk, butter, eggs, and brown sugar. Add the sweet potatoes and stir well to combine.

4 In a separate large bowl, mix together the flour, baking powder, and salt. Stir the sweet potato mixture into the flour mixture and mix well to combine.

5 Spray the waffle iron with nonstick cooking spray. Add about ⅔ cup of batter to cover the cooking surface of the iron. Close and cook the waffles until crisp and brown, about 2 to 3 minutes each. Loosely cover waffles with foil and place in the oven while preparing the remaining waffles. Serve hot topped with Honey Butter and maple syrup.

Makes 6 to 8 standard waffles

2 medium unpeeled orange-flesh sweet potatoes, washed and scrubbed

¼ cup whole milk

4 tablespoons (½ stick) unsalted butter, melted

2 large eggs, lightly beaten

3 tablespoons light brown sugar

2 cups all-purpose flour

2 teaspoons baking powder

½ teaspoon salt

Honey Butter, for serving (recipe follows)

Maple syrup, for serving

Honey Butter

Whisk the butter, honey, and salt together in a small bowl until blended well. Taste and add more honey and salt, if desired. Spoon into a serving dish, cover with plastic wrap, and refrigerate until ready to use.

Makes about ½ cup

8 tablespoons (1 stick) unsalted butter, softened

¼ cup honey

Pinch of salt

Baked Cheese Grits

4 cups water

1 teaspoon salt

1 cup quick-cooking grits

¼ teaspoon ground black pepper

4 tablespoons (½ stick) unsalted butter

1 cup grated sharp cheddar cheese

1 cup grated Monterey Jack cheese

½ cup whole milk

2 large eggs

*m*y fondest memory as a child was waking up to my father's cheese grits . . . and biscuits with molasses.
—Shakara

1 Preheat the oven to 350°F. Generously butter an 8-inch casserole.

2 In a medium saucepan, bring the water and salt to a boil. Gradually whisk in the grits and reduce heat to low. Cover and simmer, stirring often, until the grits begin to thicken, about 8 minutes. Remove from heat and stir in the pepper and butter.

3 In a small bowl, mix the cheeses together. Add two-thirds of the cheeses to the grits, stirring well to melt. Whisk together the milk and eggs in separate small bowl and quickly whisk into the grits.

4 Pour the grits into the prepared casserole and sprinkle with the remaining cheese. Bake until the grits are set and firm to touch in center, about 50 minutes. Remove from the oven and let stand for 10 minutes before serving.

Makes 6 to 8 servings

Easy Coffee Cake Muffins

1 Preheat the oven to 350°F. Line two 12-cup muffin pans with paper cupcake liners.

2 Combine the flour, ¾ cup sugar, baking powder, and salt in a medium bowl.

3 Remove ½ cup of the flour mixture to a small bowl and stir in the remaining 2 tablespoons of sugar and the cinnamon. Using a fork, cut the vegetable shortening into this flour mixture until the mixture resembles coarse crumbs. Set the crumb topping mixture aside.

4 Stir together the egg, milk, and vanilla in a small bowl and add to the remaining flour mixture, whisking just until combined.

4 Using a ¼-cup measuring cup, divide the batter evenly among the muffin cups. Smooth the surface of the batter with the back of a small spoon or a silicone spatula. Evenly pour the melted butter over each of the muffins and top each with the crumb topping mixture.

5 Bake until the crumb topping is golden and a toothpick inserted into the center of each muffin comes out clean, 20 to 25 minutes. Place on a wire rack to cool slightly before serving.

Makes 24 muffins

2 cups all-purpose flour

¾ cup plus 2 tablespoons sugar

1 tablespoon baking powder

½ teaspoon salt

1 teaspoon ground cinnamon

½ cup vegetable shortening

1 large egg, slightly beaten

¾ cup whole milk

½ teaspoon vanilla extract

2 tablespoons unsalted butter, melted

Maple Pecan Crumble
French Toast Casserole

2 medium French baguettes

8 large eggs

1 cup heavy cream

2 cups whole milk

1 teaspoon vanilla extract

¼ teaspoon ground cinnamon

¼ teaspoon fresh grated nutmeg

⅛ teaspoon salt

Maple Pecan Crumble Topping
(recipe follows)

Maple syrup, for serving

*W*hat can we say about this dish—it is over-the-top delicious! If a good impression is what you want to make, you're going to have a hard time trying to top this. Start this dish the evening before your brunch, as it needs to be refrigerated overnight.

1 Butter a 9 x 13-inch baking dish. Slice the baguette on an angle into 16 one-inch slices. Save the ends of the baguette to use at a later date for bread crumbs. Arrange the bread slices in the baking dish, overlapping the slices if necessary. In a large bowl, whisk together the eggs, cream, milk, vanilla, cinnamon, nutmeg, and salt until blended well. Pour the egg mixture over the bread slices, making sure all of the bread is covered. Cover with aluminum foil and refrigerate for at least 5 hours, preferably overnight.

2 When ready to bake, preheat the oven to 350°F. Remove the casserole from the refrigerator and allow to sit out for 15 minutes. Top with the Maple Pecan Crumble Topping and bake until puffy and lightly golden, about 45 minutes. Serve with maple syrup.

Makes 8–10 servings

2 cups light brown sugar,
packed tightly

1 cup chopped pecans

8 tablespoons (1 stick) unsalted
butter, softened

2 tablespoons maple syrup

¼ teaspoon ground cinnamon

¼ teaspoon fresh grated nutmeg

Maple Pecan Crumble Topping

Pulse the brown sugar, pecans, butter, maple syrup, cinnamon, and nutmeg in a food processor just until combined.

Makes about 2 cups

Scrambled Eggs with Butter and Chives

*i*f you are thinking, "Who needs a recipe for scrambled eggs?" you would be surprised. The butter and chives are a welcome addition to ordinary eggs.

In a medium bowl, whisk together the eggs, half-and-half, chives, salt, and pepper until well blended. Melt the butter in a medium skillet over medium-low heat. Pour in the egg mixture and gently stir with a silicone spatula. Cook, stirring occasionally, until the eggs are fluffy and set. Remove from heat and spoon into a serving dish to avoid overcooking.

Makes 4 to 6 servings

6 large eggs

¼ cup half-and-half

¼ cup minced fresh chives

½ teaspoon salt

¼ teaspoon ground black pepper

6 tablespoons (¾ stick) unsalted butter

Hilton's Hash Browns

¼ cup extra virgin olive oil

2 medium onions, sliced

1 small green bell pepper, diced

1 small red bell pepper, diced

6 large Russet potatoes, peeled and sliced into ½-inch rounds

1 teaspoon seasoned salt

¼ teaspoon ground black pepper

½ teaspoon all-purpose seasoning (recommended: Goya Adobo)

½ teaspoon paprika

*m*ornings at my parents' house are not complete without my stepfather's Hash Browns! — *Shakara*

1 Heat the olive oil in a large skillet over medium heat. Add the onions and bell peppers to the skillet and cook, stirring often until the onions are tender, about 5 minutes. Add the potatoes, seasoned salt, pepper, and all-purpose seasoning. Toss the potatoes to coat with oil and seasoning and cover with a lid. Cook for 8 to 10 minutes.

2 Flip with a metal spatula, making sure not to break up the potatoes. Turn the heat up to medium-high and cook, uncovered, for 10 minutes more. Remove from the heat and sprinkle with paprika before serving.

Makes 4 to 6 servings

Bangin' Buttermilk Biscuits

*b*eing three city girls with Southern roots, we often get tested on our sweet tea, grits, and biscuit-making skills—and of course we are never scared of a challenge. These are light, fluffy, and so delicious. Enjoy!

1 Preheat the oven to 425°F. Line a baking sheet with parchment paper.

2 Sift together the flour, baking powder, and sugar into a large bowl. Using a fork, blend the shortening and chilled butter into the flour mixture until the largest pieces are the size of small peas. Make a well in the center of the flour mixture and pour in the buttermilk; stir just until the dough comes together.

3 Turn the dough out onto a lightly floured surface. With floured hands, gently fold the dough over itself six times, and pat it out to ¾-inch thickness. Using a 3-inch round biscuit cutter, cut out 12 rounds and place on the prepared baking sheet. Brush the tops of the biscuits with melted butter. Bake for 12 to 15 minutes. Serve hot with additional butter, jellies, and honey.

Makes 12 biscuits

3 cups self-rising flour, plus extra for shaping

3 teaspoons baking powder

2 teaspoons confectioners' sugar

¼ cup vegetable shortening

4 tablespoons (½ stick) unsalted butter, chilled

1¼ cups buttermilk

4 tablespoons (½ stick) unsalted butter, melted

Butter, jellies, and honey, for serving

Cream Scones

2 cups all-purpose flour, plus more for shaping

¼ cup sugar, plus more for sprinkling

1 tablespoon baking powder

½ teaspoon salt

6 tablespoons (¾ stick) unsalted butter, chilled

⅓ cup heavy cream, plus more for brushing

2 large eggs, lightly beaten

We had an interview in Philadelphia at 100.3 The Beat, and we made these for the morning show hosts Pooch and Laiya. They devoured the scones, which have been a hit ever since! Serve with apple or honey butter and watch how fast they disappear.

1 Preheat the oven to 400°F. Line a baking sheet with parchment paper.

2 Sift together the flour, ¼ cup sugar, the baking powder, and salt into a large bowl. Using a fork, blend the butter into the flour mixture until the largest pieces are the size of small peas. Whisk together the cream and eggs in a small bowl. Make a well in the center of the flour mixture and pour in the cream mixture. Stir just until the dough comes together.

3 Turn the dough out onto a lightly floured work surface. With floured hands, gently fold the dough over itself 10 times, and pat it out to ¾-inch thickness. Cut the dough into 3-inch squares with a knife and then cut each square in half to form triangles. Place on the prepared baking sheet. Brush the top of each scone with additional cream and sprinkle with sugar. Bake until the tops are golden brown, about 20 minutes.

Makes 8 scones

Picnic for Two

Day at the Beach
Overnight Buttermilk Fried Chicken
Picnic Potato Salad
Butterscotch Blondies
Sparkling Lemonade

Central Park Affair
Cold Sesame Noodles with Chicken and Asian Vegetables
Chocolate Kiss Wontons
Mint Iced Green Tea

Rainy Day Indoor Picnic
Curried Chicken Salad on Ciabatta
Kettle-Cooked Homemade Potato Chips
Red Velvet Sandwich Cakes
Lip-Puckering Strawberry Lemonade

*t*here is something about eating outdoors. The food tastes better and the atmosphere just seems more relaxing. So with that in mind—it's picnic time! Whether you're spending the day at the beach or under your favorite tree at the park, turn off your cell phone, pack up some of the delicious and easy dishes we've created, and take them outside.

Picnicking is a fun and inexpensive way to spend intimate time with your love interest, provided you've made sure to layer on the bug repellent. Ladies, there is nothing better than sprawling across a soft blanket with a good book and the man you care about by your side—and if you can get him to rub your bare feet under the warm sun while you sip on a glass of ice-cold lemonade—whew, you might need more than SPF protection for your alfresco date. Don't fret if the weatherman won't cooperate with your plans—just get creative and bring the picnic indoors.

Besides three delicious and filling menus, we've offered up a few tips on making sure your picnic for two is a successful one.

Picnic baskets are cute, but insulated coolers are safer!

Keeping cold foods cold is important when planning an outdoors meal. Keep cold foods refrigerated until you're just ready to pull out and pack them with ice packs or resealable plastic bags filled with ice in an insulated cooler. When transporting your cooler, if you are driving, store the cooler in the air-conditioned car, not in the trunk. Also, throw away any food that has been out of the cooler for more than an hour. There is nothing worse than a romantic date ending at the emergency room. Trust us.

Freeze drinks the night before.

Not only will this help with keeping your food chilled, but as they melt, you'll have frosty cold drinks to last through the day.

Find the perfect spot!

You know the saying: the early bird catches the worm—so get out early! Pick a spot with just the right amount of shade and privacy. It's hard to "snuggle" with your sweetie when the volleyball of the family of four parked right beside you keeps falling into your lap every two minutes.

Bugs love potato salad, too!

And they also love your perfume and cologne—so don't wear any. A couple of layers of Skin So Soft will help keep them off you and a citronella candle will help keep them off your blanket.

Get 'Em Girls' Picnic for Two Checklist:
A cozy blanket
Insect repellent and citronella candles
Silverware, napkins, paper plates and cups, and serving utensils

Media player with small speakers

Sanitizing gel and wet napkins

Scrabble, Uno, or a deck of cards

Condoms (Hey, you never know!)

Sunscreen

Garbage bags

Corkscrew or bottle opener

Condiments (Stop at the deli and grab a handful of extra ketchup, salt, and pepper packets.)

Antihistamine (allergy medicine)

Overnight Buttermilk Fried Chicken

*W*hether hot, at room temperature, or cold, fried chicken is the perfect picnic food—the secret to this extremely moist and flavorful chicken is the brine. This recipe takes a little time, but is truly worth it!

1 To make the brine: In a large glass or nonreactive bowl, dissolve the kosher salt in the cold water. Place the chicken in the brine solution, making sure the chicken is covered completely. Cover with plastic wrap and refrigerate overnight.

2 Drain the chicken completely and place back in the same bowl. Season with 1 teaspoon Essential Seasoning and ½ teaspoon pepper, and pour the buttermilk over the chicken. Cover again with plastic wrap and refrigerate for 30 minutes. After 30 minutes, drain the chicken in a colander and discard the buttermilk.

3 Pour the flour into a resealable plastic bag and season with the remaining Essential Seasoning, salt, and pepper. Place the chicken pieces into the bag and shake until all of the chicken is coated thoroughly. Remove the chicken from the bag and place on a platter while the oil heats.

4 Pour enough vegetable oil into a cast-iron skillet so that it comes up the sides about halfway. Heat over medium-high heat until the oil reaches a temperature of 325°F. In batches, carefully add the chicken pieces, making sure not to overcrowd the skillet. Fry the chicken, uncovered, turning occasionally, until golden brown on all sides and cooked throughout, about 8 minutes for breasts and wings and 10 minutes for thighs and legs.

5 Remove the chicken from the skillet and drain on a paper towel–lined platter. Season with additional salt and pepper and serve immediately or allow to cool completely and then wrap in parchment paper to serve later.

Makes 4 servings

BRINE
¼ cup kosher salt

4 cups cold water

One 3-pound chicken, cut into 8 pieces

2 teaspoons Get 'Em Girl Essential Seasoning (page 16)

1 teaspoon ground black pepper

2 cups buttermilk

1½ cups all-purpose flour

¼ teaspoon salt

Vegetable oil, for frying

Picnic Potato Salad

2 pounds unpeeled small white potatoes, washed, scrubbed, and cut in half

¼ cup extra virgin olive oil

3 tablespoons cider vinegar

1 tablespoon Dijon mustard

1 tablespoon honey

½ teaspoon salt

¼ teaspoon ground black pepper

½ small red onion, minced

1 tablespoon minced green bell pepper

1 teaspoon chopped fresh flat-leaf parsley

1 Place the potatoes in a pot and cover with water. Bring to a boil and cook until the potatoes are fork tender, about 8 minutes.

2 Drain the potatoes in a colander and place in a medium bowl to cool.

3 In a small bowl, whisk together the olive oil, vinegar, mustard, honey, salt, and pepper. Pour the dressing mixture over the potatoes and stir in the onions, bell pepper, and parsley. Refrigerate until ready to serve.

Makes 4 to 6 servings

Butterscotch Blondies

1 Preheat the oven to 350°F. Butter an 8-inch square baking dish liberally and line the bottom with parchment paper.

2 Sift together the flour, baking powder, and salt into a medium bowl.

3 Place the butter and brown sugar in a separate medium bowl. Beat with an electric mixer on medium speed until fluffy, about 4 minutes. Add the eggs, one at a time, and the vanilla; mix until combined well.

4 Reduce the speed to low and gradually add the flour mixture. Continue mixing until combined, scraping down the sides of the bowl as necessary. Stir in the butterscotch and toffee chips with a wooden spoon. Spread the batter in the prepared pan with a silicone spatula.

5 Bake 20 to 25 minutes, until golden brown and a toothpick inserted into the center of the blondies comes out with only a few crumbs. Remove and let cool completely in the pan before cutting into squares.

Makes 16 blondies

1¼ cups all-purpose flour

1 teaspoon baking powder

½ teaspoon salt

8 tablespoons (1 stick) unsalted butter, softened

1 cup light brown sugar, packed tightly

2 large eggs

½ teaspoon vanilla extract

⅓ cup butterscotch chips

¼ cup toffee chips

Sparkling Lemonade

Juice of 8 large lemons
(about 1 cup)

1 cup sugar

3 cups cold water

1 liter club soda, chilled

Ice cubes

Lemon wedges, for garnish

1 In a large pitcher, combine the lemon juice and sugar. Stir to dissolve the sugar. Stir in the cold water and refrigerate until ready to serve.

2 When ready to serve, add the club soda. Serve over ice, garnished with lemon wedges.

Makes about 2 quarts

Cold Sesame Noodles with Chicken and Asian Vegetables

1 Bring a large pot of lightly salted water to a boil over high heat. Stir in the noodles and bring back to a boil. Reduce the heat to a simmer and cook until the noodles are tender, about 3 minutes. Drain in a colander and rinse with cold water. Transfer the noodles to a large bowl and toss with the sesame oil.

2 In a blender with the motor running, drop in the garlic and ginger and blend. Add the peanut butter, soy sauce, brown sugar, vinegar, and red pepper flakes and pulse to combine. Slowly add the water and continue to pulse until the sauce is smooth and creamy.

3 Pour the peanut sauce over the noodles and add the cucumber and chicken. Toss to coat noodles thoroughly and serve topped with the scallions and sesame seeds.

Makes 4 servings

One 13-ounce package soba noodles

2 tablespoons toasted sesame oil

1 clove garlic

½ teaspoon peeled, minced fresh ginger

½ cup creamy peanut butter

¼ cup soy sauce

2 tablespoons light brown sugar

1 tablespoon rice wine vinegar

¼ teaspoon crushed red pepper flakes

¼ cup hot water

1 English cucumber, halved lengthwise and thinly sliced

1 cup shredded cooked chicken

4 scallions, thinly sliced

¼ cup toasted sesame seeds

Chocolate Kiss Wontons

16 square wonton skins

16 milk chocolate kiss candies

4 cups vegetable oil

Confectioners' sugar, for dusting

*t*hese are great alone or with your favorite ice cream.

1 Lay the wonton skins out on a flat surface and, one at a time, brush the edges with water. Place a chocolate kiss in the center of the wonton skin. Gather the edges of the wonton skin together to make a bundle and press together well to seal completely and cover the chocolate. Continue with the remaining wonton skins and chocolate.

2 Heat the oil in a deep pot to 350°F. Working in batches, carefully drop the wontons into the oil, making sure not to overcrowd the pot. Fry, turning often, until golden brown. Using a slotted spoon, remove the wontons from the oil and place on a paper towel–lined platter. Dust liberally with powdered sugar and serve immediately.

Makes 4 to 6 servings

Mint Iced Green Tea

In a large saucepan, bring the water to a boil. Remove from the heat and add the mint leaves and tea bags. Cover and steep for 15 minutes. Strain the tea into a large pitcher and add the honey, sugar, and lemon juice. Refrigerate until cold and serve over ice.

Makes 6 servings

6 cups water

½ cup mint leaves, loosely packed

6 green tea bags

¼ cup honey

½ cup sugar

1 tablespoon fresh lemon juice

Ice cubes

Curried Chicken Salad on Ciabatta

3 cups cooked and diced (1 inch) boneless, skinless chicken breast

¾ cup finely diced celery (about 3 medium stalks)

1 small red onion, finely diced

2 tablespoons prepared mango chutney

1 teaspoon salt

1 cup mayonnaise

1 teaspoon mild curry powder

2 ounces baby arugula, washed and dried thoroughly

1 large loaf ciabatta bread

*W*e did a picnic-themed cooking demo on the CN8 network in Philadelphia, PA, and this recipe was an absolute hit with the host.

1 In a large bowl, combine the chicken, celery, onions, mango chutney, salt, mayonnaise, and curry powder. Mix until well combined. Cover with plastic wrap and refrigerate until ready to serve.

2 Once you're ready to serve, preheat the oven to 400°F. Slice the ciabatta in half horizontally and separate the top from the bottom. Toast the bread in the oven, cut side up, for 5 to 7 minutes; cool slightly. Place half the arugula on the bottom piece of bread and then layer with the chicken salad; finish with another layer of arugula. Place the top slice of ciabatta on top and cut in thirds crosswise. Serve at room temperature.

Makes 3 servings

Kettle-Cooked Homemade Potato Chips

i absolutely love kettle-cooked chips! My mom would eat them when I was a kid and I remember vividly the loud crunch with each bite. I also remember that she didn't share them with me very often! —*Jeniece*

1 Dry the potato slices on a baking sheet between layers of paper towels to make sure they are very dry before frying.

2 Heat about 3 inches of oil in a deep fryer or a large heavy pot until the temperature reaches 400°F. Fry the potatoes in small batches until golden brown on both sides, turning once. Remove with a slotted spoon and place on a dry paper towel–lined baking sheet to drain. Season with salt immediately and serve at room temperature.

Makes 4 to 6 servings

6 large Russet potatoes, peeled and sliced lengthwise into ⅛-inch-thick slices

Peanut oil, for deep frying

Salt

Red Velvet Sandwich Cakes

CAKES

1 cup sugar

8 tablespoons (1 stick) unsalted butter, softened

1 large egg

1 tablespoon Dutch-process cocoa powder

1½ teaspoons red food coloring

1½ cups all-purpose flour

1 teaspoon baking powder

½ teaspoon salt

½ cup buttermilk

1 teaspoon vanilla extract

¼ teaspoon baking soda

1½ teaspoons white vinegar

FILLING

1 cup milk

5 tablespoons all-purpose flour

½ cup mascarpone cheese, softened

½ cup cream cheese, softened

8 tablespoons (1 stick) unsalted butter, softened

½ cup marshmallow crème

½ teaspoon vanilla extract

¼ teaspoon almond extract

1 cup confectioners' sugar

½ cup crushed toasted pecans

1 Preheat the oven to 375°F. Line two baking sheets with parchment paper.

2 Beat together the sugar and butter in a large bowl using an electric mixer on high speed until light and fluffy, about 2 minutes. Add the egg and mix well. In a small bowl, mix the cocoa and red food coloring together. Add to the sugar mixture. Mix well.

3 Sift together the flour, baking powder, and salt into a large bowl. With the electric mixer on low, slowly add the flour mixture to the sugar mixture alternately with the buttermilk; blend in the vanilla. Combine the baking soda and vinegar in a small bowl and add to the mixture. Drop the batter 2 tablespoonfuls at a time onto the prepared parchment paper.

4 Bake until the tops spring back when pressed lightly in the center and the edges just begin to brown, about 10 minutes. Remove from baking sheets and cool completely on the parchment before filling.

5 To make the filling: Pour the milk into a small saucepan over medium heat. Slowly whisk in the flour, making sure to work out any lumps. Cook, whisking constantly, until the mixture begins to get very thick and stiff. Remove from heat and spoon into a small bowl to cool completely.

6 Meanwhile, using an electric mixer on high speed, blend the mascarpone, cream cheese, and butter together in a large bowl until smooth. Lower the mixer speed and add the marshmallow crème, vanilla and almond extracts, and confectioners' sugar. Blend just until combined. Add the cooled flour mixture and whip just until fluffy.

7 To assemble the cakes: Spread some filling onto the bottom side of a cake and top with another cake to make a sandwich. Wrap individually in plastic wrap and refrigerate until ready to serve.

Makes 20 sandwich cakes

Lip-Puckering Strawberry Lemonade

1 In a large pitcher, combine the lemon juice and sugar, stirring to dissolve the sugar.

2 Puree the strawberries in a blender. Add to the lemon juice mixture. Add the cold water and blend well. Serve over ice, garnished with slices of lemon and whole strawberries.

Makes about 2 quarts

Juice of 8 large lemons (about 1 cup)

1 cup sugar

1 pint fresh strawberries, hulled and cut in half

7 cups cold water

Ice cubes

Lemon slices or wedges, for garnish

Whole strawberries, for garnish

First Holiday

Thanksgiving Dinner for Two
Turkey Tenderloins with Cornbread Stuffing
Whole Cranberry Relish
Candied Pecan Sweet Potato Wedges
Southern-Style Green Beans with Sweet Onion Dressing
Bourbon Pecan Pie Cupcakes with Vanilla Bean Glaze

Christmas Feast at Your Place
Deep-Fried Turkey
Holiday Glazed Ham
Southern Girls' Sage Sausage Dressing
Braised Mixed Greens with Smoked Turkey
Mashed Sweet Potatoes
Four-Cheese Macaroni and Cheese with a Kick!
Cookie's Sweet Potato Pie
Grandma Adean's Pecan Millionnaires

New Year's Eve Dinner Party
Pork Roast with Mushroom Gravy
Hoppin' John
Sautéed Kale
Pineapple-Layered Cake

*Y*ou just closed on your new home, and you are excited about hosting this year's holiday dinner. You send out thirty invitations, receive thirty RSVPs—and you quickly realize that you were crazy for thinking your family would pass on a free meal and that you are in over your head.

Don't worry—whether you're making a Thanksgiving dinner for two, or a Christmas dinner for twenty, the Get 'Em Girls have got you covered. If you need to, just mix and match recipes and work it out!

Turkey Tenderloins with Cornbread Stuffing

1 Preheat the oven to 375°F. Spray a shallow baking dish with nonstick cooking spray.

2 Cut a pocket lengthwise along the thickest side of the tenderloins. Stuff each tenderloin with about 1 cup of stuffing and wrap with cooking twine or secure with toothpicks.

3 In a small bowl, mix together the salt, pepper, and poultry seasoning. Drizzle the olive oil and melted butter over the turkey tenderloins and rub in; season with the salt mixture and place in the prepared baking dish.

4 Bake uncovered for 1 hour, or until the tenderloins reach an internal temperature of 170°F on an instant-read thermometer.

Makes about 4 servings

2 pounds turkey breast tenderloins

2 cups Easy Cornbread Stuffing (recipe follows)

1 tablespoon salt

1½ teaspoons ground black pepper

1 teaspoon poultry seasoning

2 tablespoons extra virgin olive oil

2 tablespoons unsalted butter, melted

Easy Cornbread Stuffing

1 Melt the butter in a medium skillet over medium heat. Add the onions and celery and cook, stirring occasionally, until the onions are soft and lightly browned, about 10 minutes.

2 In a large bowl, combine the corn muffin pieces, onion and celery mixture, poultry seasoning, sage, and salt and pepper. Toss to mix well.

3 In a small bowl, whisk together the egg, half-and-half, and chicken stock. Pour the egg mixture over the corn muffin mixture and stir together until well combined. Stuff the cavity of the turkey.

Makes 4 cups

2 tablespoons unsalted butter

1 large sweet onion, chopped (recommended: Vidalia)

¼ cup chopped celery (about 1 stalk)

6 large corn muffins, cubed

½ teaspoon poultry seasoning

½ teaspoon dried sage

Salt and ground black pepper

1 large egg

¼ cup half-and-half

¼ cup chicken broth

VARIATION

If you are not stuffing a turkey or tenderloin, spoon the stuffing mixture into a buttered shallow baking dish and bake at 375°F until the top is golden brown and crusty, about 30 minutes.

Whole Cranberry Relish

2 cups fresh or frozen whole cranberries

½ cup sugar

3 tablespoons orange juice

Grated peel of 1 orange

Combine all the ingredients in a small saucepan. Bring to a boil, then lower to a simmer. Continue to cook for 10 to 15 minutes until the mixture is thick and the berries are glazed. Allow to cool. Transfer to a covered container and refrigerate until needed.

Makes about 2 cups

Candied Pecan Sweet Potato Wedges

1 Preheat the oven to 375°F. Spray a 9 by 13-inch baking dish with nonstick cooking spray.

2 Quarter the sweet potatoes lengthwise and place in the baking dish. Drizzle with melted butter and toss to coat. In a small bowl, mix together the brown sugar, pecans, cinnamon, nutmeg, allspice, and salt. Pour the brown sugar mixture over the sweet potatoes and toss to coat thoroughly. Drizzle the maple syrup over the potatoes.

3 Bake until the sweet potatoes are fork tender and glazed, 35 to 40 minutes.

Makes 4 servings

4 large unpeeled orange-flesh sweet potatoes, washed and scrubbed

4 tablespoons (½ stick) unsalted butter, melted

1 cup light brown sugar

½ cup chopped pecans

1 teaspoon ground cinnamon

¼ teaspoon freshly grated nutmeg

¼ teaspoon ground allspice

¼ teaspoon salt

¼ cup maple syrup

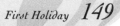

Southern-Style Green Beans with Sweet Onion Dressing

Salt

½ pound fresh green beans

½ cup Sweet Onion Dressing (recipe follows)

Bring a small saucepan of salted water to a boil. Place the green beans in the water and cook until just tender, about 7 minutes. Drain the beans and toss in a medium bowl with the dressing. Serve immediately.

Makes 2 servings

1 cup sugar

1 teaspoon salt

¼ teaspoon dry mustard

¼ teaspoon celery seed

1 medium Vidalia or other sweet onion, grated

2 tablespoons vegetable oil

½ cup white vinegar

Sweet Onion Dressing

Combine all the ingredients in a small saucepan. Cook over medium-low heat, stirring occasionally, until the sugar is melted. Cool and refrigerate, or serve as a warm dressing. (Refrigerate remaining dressing for up to 5 days.)

Makes about 1½ cups

Bourbon Pecan Pie Cupcakes with Vanilla Bean Glaze

*W*e made these for an event that *Essence* magazine held for Tyra Banks, and they have been in our arsenal of goodness ever since.

1 Preheat the oven to 350°F. Line the bottoms of two 12-cup muffin pans with parchment circles and spray the inside of the cups with non-stick cooking spray.

2 Spread the pecans on a baking sheet and roast until toasted, about 7 minutes. Remove and allow them to cool before chopping coarsely. Meanwhile, combine the butter, corn syrup, brown sugar, and salt in a medium saucepan. Cook, stirring constantly, until the butter and brown sugar melt and the mixture is smooth. Remove from heat and stir in the bourbon and pecans. Set aside.

3 To make the cupcakes: Sift the flour, baking powder, baking soda, and salt together into a medium bowl. In a large bowl, beat the eggs and sugar together with an electric mixer on medium speed, until thickened and lightened, about 2 minutes. Add the oil and vanilla extract and continue to mix. Add the sour cream and mix until no white streaks remain. Reduce speed to low and slowly beat in the flour mixture until the batter is smooth.

4 Spoon 2 tablespoons of the pecan topping in the bottom of each muffin cup and fill each one three-quarters full with cupcake batter.

5 Bake until a toothpick inserted into the cupcake only comes out clean, about 25 minutes. Remove and allow the cupcakes to cool for 3 minutes before carefully flipping them over onto a wire rack set on top of a baking sheet. Allow to cool completely before covering with vanilla bean glaze.

6 To make the glaze: Split the vanilla bean lengthwise and scrape the seeds into a small bowl. Whisk in the confectioners' sugar and cream until the glaze reaches the consistency of pancake batter. Lightly drizzle over the top of cooled cupcakes.

Makes 24 cupcakes

TIP

Place the vanilla bean pod in a container with a tight-fitting lid and fill with 2 cups of granulated sugar. Allow to sit for 2 weeks for delicious vanilla sugar to use in your favorite dessert recipes!

TOPPING

1½ cups pecan halves

8 tablespoons (1 stick) unsalted butter

5 tablespoons light corn syrup

⅔ cup light brown sugar

⅛ teaspoon salt

1 tablespoon bourbon

CUPCAKES

2½ cups unbleached all-purpose flour

1 teaspoon baking powder

½ teaspoon baking soda

½ teaspoon salt

3 large eggs

2 cups granulated sugar

1 cup vegetable oil

2 teaspoons vanilla extract

1 cup sour cream

VANILLA BEAN GLAZE

1 vanilla bean

1 cup confectioners' sugar

3 tablespoons heavy cream

Deep-Fried Turkey

One 10- to 12-pound turkey

8 tablespoons (1 stick) unsalted butter

2 tablespoons poultry seasoning

2 tablespoons hot pepper sauce

2 teaspoons garlic powder

2 teaspoons onion powder

1 teaspoon ground black pepper

1 bay leaf

SPECIAL TOOLS

Turkey Fryer Flavor injector

3 to 5 gallons peanut oil

*M*y mom makes fried turkeys for us and half of the congregation of her church every Thanksgiving and Christmas holiday—needless to say, this is her delicious recipe.—*Jeniece*

1 Wash the turkey inside and out, place on a rack in a large roasting pan, pat dry with paper towels, and allow to drain.

2 Combine the butter, poultry seasoning, hot pepper sauce, garlic and onion powders, black pepper, and bay leaf in a small saucepan over medium-high heat. Cook uncovered until the sauce begins to reduce and the color deepens, about 10 minutes. Allow the sauce to cool before injecting it into the turkey, making sure to rub in any sauce that has dripped down into the pan. Let turkey come to room temperature while you prepare the turkey fryer.

3 Heat peanut oil in a turkey fryer according to the manufacturer's instructions to 350°F. Carefully lower the turkey into the hot oil, making sure it is fully submerged. Fry the turkey for 4 minutes per pound plus 5 minutes for the bird; the internal temperature of the turkey should read between 170° and 180°F on an instant-read thermometer. Remove the turkey from the oil and set the turkey stand in a roasting pan lined with paper towels to drain the excess oil. Let the turkey rest for 15 minutes so the juices settle before carving.

Makes 6 to 8 servings

TIP

Before you begin, measure how much oil you'll need to fry the turkey by placing your turkey in the basket or hanger included with the fryer and cover it with water. Remove the turkey and mark the water surface level. Dry turkey and fryer thoroughly before adding the oil.

FOR YOUR SAFETY, never fry a turkey indoors, and follow the manufacturer's instructions for your fryer.

Holiday Glazed Ham

1 Preheat the oven to 325°F.

2 Place ham bone side down or skin side up in a shallow baking pan, pour the ginger ale over the ham, and cover loosely with aluminum foil. Bake, basting occasionally, for 1 hour.

3 Meanwhile, mix together the preserves, honey, cornstarch, lemon juice, and cloves in a small saucepan and warm over medium heat until the preserves have melted, about 3 minutes. Remove from heat and set aside.

4 After 1 hour of cooking, remove the ham from the oven, uncover, and allow the ham to cool enough to handle. With a sharp knife, make shallow crisscross cuts all over the fatty side of the ham, scoring 1-inch squares. Pour the glaze over the top and let it drip down the ham. Place the ham back in the oven uncovered and bake for another 30 minutes. Remove from oven and let stand 15 minutes before slicing.

Makes 8 to 10 servings

One 5- to 7-pound bone-in partially cooked cured ham, butt portion

2 cups ginger ale

½ cup apricot preserves

½ cup honey

1 tablespoon cornstarch

3 tablespoons lemon juice

¼ teaspoon ground cloves

Southern Girls' Sage Sausage Dressing

2 tablespoons unsalted butter

1 large sweet onion, chopped
(recommended: Vidalia)

¼ cup chopped celery
(about 1 stalk)

6 large corn muffins, cubed

½ pound mild bulk sage sausage,
cooked and drained

½ teaspoon poultry seasoning

½ teaspoon dried sage

Salt and ground black pepper

1 large egg

¼ cup half-and-half

¼ cup chicken broth

1 Preheat the oven to 375°F. Butter an 8-inch square baking dish.

2 Melt the butter in a medium skillet over medium heat. Add the onions and celery and cook, stirring occasionally, until the onions are soft and lightly browned, about 10 minutes.

3 In a large bowl, combine the corn muffin pieces, the onion and celery mixture, cooked sausage, poultry seasoning, sage, and salt and pepper. Toss to mix well.

4 In a small bowl, whisk together the egg, half and half, and chicken stock. Pour the egg mixture over the corn muffin and sausage mixture and stir together until well combined. Spoon the mixture into the prepared baking dish. Bake until the top is golden brown and crusty, about 30 minutes.

Makes 4 cups

Braised Mixed Greens with Smoked Turkey

1 Place the turkey wings and Essential Seasoning in a large saucepan and cover with water. Bring to a boil over medium-high heat and cook until tender, about 1 hour. Remove turkey wings from the pot and allow to cool. Once cool, remove skin, cut up, and set aside.

2 Meanwhile, wash the mustard and turnip greens thoroughly in a sink full of cold water and drain in a colander. Lay the leaves out flat on top of each other, roll together, and slice into 1-inch pieces.

3 Add the greens to the pot, along with the cooled, cut-up turkey wings and more water, if needed, to cover the greens. Add the salt, pepper, sugar, and red pepper flakes. Reduce heat to low and cover. Simmer until greens are tender, about 30 to 45 minutes and serve.

Makes 6 to 8 servings

2 smoked turkey wings, cut up

1 teaspoon Get 'Em Girl Essential Seasoning (page 16)

2 pounds mustard greens, chopped

1 pound turnip greens, chopped

1 teaspoon salt

1 teaspoon ground black pepper

1½ teaspoons sugar

½ teaspoon crushed red pepper flakes

Mashed Sweet Potatoes

3 medium unpeeled orange-flesh sweet potatoes

½ cup half-and-half

3 tablespoons unsalted butter, softened

3 tablespoons light brown sugar

1 teaspoon ground cinnamon

¼ teaspoon freshly grated nutmeg

¼ teaspoon salt

1 Bring a large pot of water to a boil over high heat. Add the sweet potatoes and cook until fork tender, about 15 to 20 minutes. Drain in a colander and rinse under cold running water until cool enough to handle. Peel the potatoes.

2 Dice the potatoes and place in a medium saucepan over low heat. Add the half-and-half, butter, brown sugar, cinnamon, nutmeg, and salt. Mash with a potato masher. Heat through, stirring constantly, and serve immediately.

Makes 4 servings

Four-Cheese Macaroni and Cheese with a Kick!

*b*ack in our online days, you could find Shakara and me feuding on our favorite Web site, and when we finally got a chance to meet face to face, we hit it off—so funny how things work out. Well, because of that same site, I met some really cool people, including Ms. SVV! When I tell you she put her foot in a pan of macaroni and cheese, it's not a lie! This is my version of her delicious dish; I hope it does hers just a little bit of justice!

—Jeniece

1 Preheat the oven to 350°F. Lightly butter a 9 by 13-inch baking dish.

2 To make the cheese sauce, in a medium saucepan melt the butter over medium-low heat. Slowly whisk in the flour until smooth, about 1 minute. Reduce heat to low and slowly add the milk, whisking until the sauce is smooth and has thickened. Add the cheddar and continue to whisk until the cheese has melted. Stir in the salt, white pepper, and nutmeg. Remove from the heat.

3 Bring a large pot of lightly salted water to a boil over high heat. Stir in the elbow macaroni and cook until the elbow macaroni is just tender, about 7 minutes. Do not overcook. Drain well in a colander and return to the pot.

4 Melt 8 tablespoons of the butter in a small saucepan and stir into the macaroni. In a large bowl, mix together the pepper Jack, sharp cheddar, and muenster cheeses. Stir 2 cups of the cheese mixture, the half-and-half, and cheese sauce into the macaroni. Stir in the eggs, Essential Seasoning, and black pepper and transfer to the prepared baking dish. Top with the remaining ½ cup of shredded cheese and dot with the remaining 2 tablespoons of butter.

5 Bake until the cheese begins to bubble around the edges, about 35 minutes.

Makes 6 to 8 servings

CHEESE SAUCE

2 tablespoons unsalted butter

2 tablespoons all-purpose flour

1 cup whole milk

½ cup grated mild cheddar cheese

½ teaspoon salt

¼ teaspoon ground white pepper

Pinch of freshly grated nutmeg

One 16-ounce package elbow macaroni

10 tablespoons (1¼ sticks) unsalted butter

1 cup grated pepper Jack cheese

¾ cup grated sharp cheddar cheese

¾ cup grated muenster cheese

2 cups half-and-half

2 large eggs, lightly beaten

½ teaspoon Get 'Em Girl Essential Seasoning (page 16)

¼ teaspoon ground black pepper

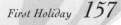

Cookie's Sweet Potato Pie

4 small to medium unpeeled orange-flesh sweet potatoes

4 tablespoons (½ stick) unsalted butter, softened

1½ cups sugar

½ teaspoon ground cinnamon

½ teaspoon ground allspice

¼ teaspoon freshly grated nutmeg

2 tablespoons self-rising flour

Dash of salt

¼ cup maple syrup

½ teaspoon vanilla extract

½ cup evaporated milk

One 9-inch unbaked pie crust, store bought

a holiday staple in all of our families is a delicious sweet potato pie. Enjoy with a dollop of freshly whipped cream.

1 Preheat the oven to 350°F.

2 Place the sweet potatoes in a large pot and fill with water to cover. Bring to a boil on medium-high heat and cook until fork tender. Drain in a colander and rinse under cold running water until cool enough to handle. Peel them and place in a large bowl.

3 Using a potato masher, mash the potatoes with the butter and sugar until combined. Stir in the cinnamon, allspice, nutmeg, flour, and salt and mix well.

4 In a small bowl, combine the maple syrup, vanilla, and milk. Slowly stir into the sweet potato mixture. Pour the batter into the pie crust and bake until the center of the pie is set and a knife inserted into the center comes out clean, about 1 hour.

Makes 6 to 8 servings

TAKE NOTE

If your crust is cooking faster than your pie filling, cover the edge of the pie crust with aluminum foil.

Grandma Adean's Pecan Millionaires

*C*hristmas without my grandmother's Pecan Millionaires is unheard of! Vanilla is my favorite. — *Shakara*

1 Preheat the oven to 325°F. Line a baking sheet with wax paper and spray with nonstick cooking spray.

2 Spread the pecans in a single layer on an unlined baking sheet and bake in the oven until toasted, about 7 minutes. Remove and transfer to a bowl to cool.

3 In a medium saucepan, combine the caramels and milk. Cook over low heat, stirring often, until the caramels have melted. Remove from heat, add the pecans, and mix until combined well. Drop the mixture by the tablespoonful onto the prepared baking sheet and refrigerate until cold, about 45 minutes.

4 When the candy is hardened and completely cold, remove from the refrigerator. In the top of a double boiler or a heatproof bowl set over a pot of simmering water, melt the chocolate, stirring occasionally, until smooth.

5 Using tongs, dip the candies in the melted chocolate to cover completely and return to the wax-paper-lined baking sheet to harden.

Makes about 20 pieces

2 cups chopped pecans

One 14-ounce bag caramels, unwrapped

One 14-ounce can sweetened condensed milk

12 ounces milk, white, or dark chocolate, chopped

Pork Roast with Mushroom Gravy

One 3-pound boneless pork loin roast

1 tablespoon Get 'Em Girl Essential Seasoning (page 16)

½ teaspoon ground black pepper

3 tablespoons vegetable oil

6 tablespoons all-purpose flour

1 large yellow onion, finely chopped

1 stalk celery, finely chopped

½ medium green bell pepper, chopped

1 tablespoon minced garlic

6 ounces white mushrooms, thinly sliced

1 quart low-sodium beef broth

1 teaspoon Worcestershire sauce

1 Season the roast evenly with 2 teaspoons of the Essential Seasoning and the pepper, rubbing into the meat. In a Dutch oven, heat the oil over medium-high until almost smoking. Add the roast to the pan and cook, turning occasionally, until the roast is evenly browned on all sides, about 6 to 8 minutes. Transfer the roast to a platter and set aside.

2 Reduce the heat to medium and add the flour. Cook, stirring constantly, until the flour has browned, making sure not to burn, about 1 to 2 minutes. Add the onions, celery, and bell peppers, and cook, stirring, until the vegetables have softened, about 5 minutes. Add the remaining Essential Seasoning and the garlic and cook until the garlic is fragrant, about 1 minute. Add the mushrooms and cook, stirring frequently, until they have released their liquid, about 4 minutes. Add the beef broth and Worcestershire and bring the sauce to a boil.

3 Return the roast to the pan and cover. Reduce the heat to low and cook for 30 minutes. Turn the roast over, cover the pan, and continue to cook on low heat until the roast is tender and has reached an internal temperature of 150°F on an instant-read thermometer, about 25 minutes.

4 Remove the roast from the pan and transfer to a platter. Cover loosely with aluminum foil and continue to cook the sauce uncovered until it is reduced and thickened, about 10 minutes. Slice the pork roast and serve with the sauce on the side.

Makes 6 to 8 servings

Hoppin' John

*i*can remember having this dish every New Year's as a child in South Carolina and the dish is still a staple for every New Year's meal. —*Jeniece*

1 Wash and sort the peas. Place them in a medium saucepan, add the water, and discard any peas that float.

2 Add the hot pepper (if using), the ham hock, and onions, and gently boil the peas, uncovered, until tender but not mushy, about 1½ hours, or until 2 cups of liquid remain.

3 Remove the ham hock from the pot and allow to cool. Add the rice to the pot, cover, and simmer over low heat for about 20 minutes, never lifting the lid. Once the ham hock is cool enough to handle, pick the meat from the bone and chop finely.

4 Remove the rice from the heat and allow to steam, still covered, for another 10 minutes. Remove the cover, fluff with a fork, stir in the ham hock meat, and serve immediately.

Makes 6 servings

1 cup small dried black-eye peas

5 cups water

1 dried hot pepper (optional)

1 smoked ham hock

1 medium onion, chopped (about ¾ cup)

1 cup long-grain white rice

Sautéed Kale

2 bunches kale (about 2 pounds), tough stem removed

3 tablespoons extra virgin olive oil

2 cloves garlic, minced

2 quarts low-sodium chicken broth

1½ teaspoons hot pepper sauce, plus extra for serving

1 teaspoon salt

½ teaspoon ground black pepper

2 teaspoons sugar

1 Stack 6 to 8 stripped kale leaves on top of each other, roll up, and cut into 1-inch slices.

2 Heat the olive oil in a large deep skillet over medium heat. Add the garlic and cook, stirring often, until the garlic is fragrant and soft, about 2 minutes. Add the greens and toss well with tongs. Stir in the chicken broth, hot pepper sauce, salt, pepper, and sugar, and cook until the greens are tender and wilted, about 1 hour. Serve with additional hot pepper sauce.

Makes 6 to 8 servings

MAKE IT
YOUR OWN

Use your favorite mixture of greens for an easy variation. Substitute aged balsamic vinegar for hot pepper sauce for an elegant and unexpected twist on a classic.

Pineapple-Layered Cake

1 Prepare the cake mix according to the package directions for 2 9-inch cake layers. Remove from pans and let cool completely on a wire rack.

2 To make the icing, mix together the crushed pineapple and instant pudding. Let mixture refrigerate for 30 minutes.

3 Next, mix sour cream into the pineapple and pudding mixture and, using a silicon spatula, fold in the whippped topping.

4 Spread icing evenly between layers and on top and sides of cooled cake.

Makes 8 servings

One 18.25-ounce box yellow cake mix

One 20-ounce can crushed pineapple (not drained), preferred Del Monte

One 6-ounce package vanilla instant pudding and pie filling

1 cup sour cream

One 8-ounce container frozen whipped topping, thawed

Light Bites with the Girls

Noshin N' Awlins-Style
Baby Arugula Salad with Honey Dijon Vinaigrette
Chicken Jambalaya
Bananas Foster Parfaits

Vegetarian Italian
Vegetable Rigatoni Bolognese
Parmesan Crisps
Spinach and Roasted Pear Salad with Pomegranate Vinaigrette

Caribbean Nights
Spicy Shrimp Curry
Jerk Chicken Salad with Orange-Honey Vinaigrette
Mango sorbet (store-bought)

*O*ur way to celebrate the start of a new diet is to go to our favorite barbecue restaurant to eat and drink until our hearts are content—this is our way of starting anew. Fast-forward two weeks later, you can usually find us at the same barbecue restaurant—starting anew, again. So if you are anything like us, we have you covered, because girlfriends can be your greatest supporters or your greatest enemies when it comes to dieting. Of course, you are probably expecting us to give some tips on dieting, but we are still trying to figure it out ourselves.

Baby Arugula Salad with Honey Dijon Vinaigrette

Place the arugula and onions in a large bowl and toss to combine. Combine the shallot, garlic, vinegar, olive oil, sugar, honey, mustard, and salt and pepper in a jar with a tight-fitting lid and shake vigorously until thickened and combined. Pour the vinaigrette over the arugula and onions and toss to coat.

Makes 4 to 6 servings

6 cups baby arugula, washed and dried thoroughly

1 small red onion, thinly sliced

1 teaspoon finely minced shallots

1 clove garlic, finely minced

2 teaspoons cider vinegar

¼ cup extra virgin olive oil

½ teaspoon sugar

1 teaspoon honey

1 teaspoon Dijon mustard

Pinch of salt and ground black pepper

Chicken Jambalaya

2 tablespoons extra virgin olive oil

1½ pounds boneless, skinless chicken breasts

½ teaspoon salt

2 tablespoons unsalted butter

1 small onion, chopped

3 cloves garlic, minced

2 stalks celery, chopped

1 medium green bell pepper, chopped

One 16-ounce can crushed tomatoes

⅔ cup uncooked long-grain white rice

½ teaspoon dried thyme

½ teaspoon dried basil

1½ teaspoons Cajun spice blend

¼ teaspoon cayenne pepper

¼ teaspoon ground black pepper

1½ cups low-sodium chicken broth

1 teaspoon hot pepper sauce

1 bay leaf

2 scallions, chopped

1 Heat the olive oil in a large saucepan or Dutch oven over medium heat. Wash and pat dry the chicken and season with salt. Add the chicken to the saucepan, stirring occasionally, until the chicken is cooked through and no pink remains. Remove the chicken, reserving the pan drippings. Chop into ½-inch pieces and set aside.

2 Add the butter to the drippings in the pan and stir in the onions, garlic, celery, and bell pepper. Cook, stirring occasionally, until the vegetables are tender, about 5 minutes. Return the chicken to the pan and stir in the tomatoes, rice, thyme, basil, Cajun spice, cayenne, black pepper, chicken broth, hot pepper sauce, and bay leaf. Reduce the heat to low and cover with a tight-fitting lid.

3 Cook until the rice is tender, about 20 minutes. Remove from heat, remove the bay leaf, stir in the scallions, and serve immediately.

Makes 4 to 6 servings

Bananas Foster Parfaits

*t*his is a lighter version of one of our favorite desserts.

1 Melt the butter in a medium saucepan over medium-low heat. Stir in the sugar substitute, rum and vanilla extracts, cinnamon, and salt and lower the heat to simmer. Cook just until the mixture begins to bubble, 1 to 2 minutes. Stir in the bananas and cook, stirring often, for 2 minutes.

2 Allow the bananas to cool slightly and begin layering in parfait glasses. Start with ¼ cup whipped topping per cup. Spoon the bananas over the topping, dividing equally. Sprinkle each with crushed gingersnaps and top with ¼ cup whipped topping. Garnish with 1 whole gingersnap and serve immediately.

Makes 4 servings

1 tablespoon unsalted butter

¼ cup brown sugar blend sugar substitute (recommended: Splenda Brown Sugar Blend)

1 teaspoon rum extract

1 teaspoon vanilla extract

½ teaspoon ground cinnamon

Pinch of salt

2 bananas, sliced

One 8-ounce container fat-free frozen whipped topping, thawed (recommended: Cool Whip Free)

½ cup sugar-free gingersnap crumbs (about 5 cookies)

4 whole sugar-free gingersnaps, for garnish

Vegetable Rigatoni Bolognese

¼ cup extra virgin olive oil

1 small onion, chopped

⅓ cup chopped carrots (about 2 carrots)

¼ cup chopped celery (about 1 stalk)

2 cloves garlic, minced

1 pound mushroom blend (shiitake, cremini, oyster), stemmed and coarsley chopped

2 tablespoons tomato paste

Salt

Ground black pepper

½ cup red wine

1 cup water

One 28-ounce can whole tomatoes, hand-crushed, with their juice

One 8-ounce can tomato sauce

½ teaspoon dried oregano

2 fresh basil leaves

One 16-ounce package whole-grain rigatoni

½ cup freshly grated Parmesan cheese

*t*his vegetarian version of our rigatoni Bolognese is full of delicious and healthful veggies and hearty mushrooms.

1 In a Dutch oven, heat the olive oil over medium heat. Add the onions, carrots, and celery. Cook, stirring often, until the vegetables are tender but not brown, about 7 minutes. Stir in the garlic and cook, stirring often, until the garlic is fragrant, about 1 minute. Add the mushrooms and tomato paste and season with 1 teaspoon salt and ½ teaspoon pepper. Cook, stirring often, until the mushrooms are softened, about 5 minutes.

2 Add the wine and cook, stirring frequently, for 10 minutes. Stir in the water, tomatoes with their juice, and tomato sauce. Add the oregano and basil. Bring to a boil, then reduce heat to low. Simmer, stirring occasionally, until the sauce is thick, 1 to 1½ hours. Remove from the heat, taste, and season with additional salt and pepper as necessary.

3 Meanwhile, bring a large pot of water to a boil. Season with salt and add the rigatoni. Cook according to the package directions until just tender. Drain in a colander and place in a large bowl. Toss the pasta with half of the sauce. Serve topped with additional sauce and Parmesan.

Makes 8 to 10 servings.

Parmesan Crisps

Whether eaten as a delicious snack with a cheesy bite or used as garnish for an elegant Italian dinner, these crisps are just as easy to make as they are to devour!

1 Preheat the oven to 350°F. Line a baking sheet with parchment paper and spray with nonstick cooking spray. Using a tablespoon, spoon the cheese into mounds on the baking sheet and flatten with the back of the spoon into 4-inch rounds.

2 Bake in batches until golden and crisp, about 4 minutes, and allow them to cool before serving.

Makes 10 to 12 crisps

2 cups coarsely grated Parmesan cheese

Spinach and Roasted Pear Salad with Pomegranate Vinaigrette

2 ounces pomegranate molasses

1 teaspoon finely minced shallots

½ cup white wine vinegar

2 teaspoons fresh lemon juice

2 tablespoons honey

1 tablespoon extra virgin olive oil

2 tablespoons walnut oil

Salt and ground black pepper

4 ounces spinach leaves, washed and dried thoroughly

2 Roasted Pears (recipe below)

¼ cup Candied Walnuts (page 173; optional)

To make the vinaigrette, combine the pomegranate molasses, shallots, vinegar, lemon juice, honey, olive oil, and walnut oil in a jar with a tight-fitting lid; season to taste with salt and pepper and shake vigorously to combine. Place the greens in a large bowl and add half of the vinaigrette, tossing to coat the leaves. Add more dressing as desired. Serve immediately with the pear slices arranged atop the greens and sprinkle each serving with Candied Walnuts, if using.

Makes 2 to 4 servings

2 Bosc pears, halved, cored, and thinly sliced lengthwise

1 teaspoon salt

¼ teaspoon ground black pepper

1 tablespoon extra virgin olive oil

Roasted Pears

Preheat the oven to 400°F.

Place the pears in a medium bowl and add the remaining ingredients. Toss well to coat and spread in a single layer on a parchment-lined baking sheet. Bake until pears are tender and golden brown, about 25 to 30 minutes.

Makes 2 to 4 servings

Candied Walnuts

1 Preheat the oven to 350°F. Line two baking sheets with parchment paper.

2 Spread the walnuts in a single layer on one of the baking sheets and bake until lightly toasted, about 6 minutes. Remove and set aside to cool completely.

3 Pour the sugar into a heavy-bottomed medium saucepan and cook, stirring often, over medium heat, until the sugar is melted and has turned a medium amber. Quickly stir in the walnuts, making sure to coat each piece with sugar.

4 Carefully spread the walnuts out with a fork on the second baking sheet, and use the fork to break apart the clusters. Sprinkle the candied nuts with salt and allow them to cool completely before serving.

Makes 1½ cups

1½ cups walnut halves

½ cup sugar

Pinch of salt

Spicy Shrimp Curry

1 pound extra large shrimp, peeled and deveined

¼ teaspoon salt

⅛ teaspoon seafood seasoning (recommended: Old Bay)

3 tablespoons extra virgin olive oil

1 tablespoon finely chopped shallots

1 small green bell pepper, thinly sliced

1 small red bell pepper, thinly sliced

1 clove garlic, minced

1½ teaspoons mild curry powder

¼ cup chicken broth

One 12-ounce can cream of coconut (recommended: Coco Lopez)

⅛ teaspoon hot chili oil, store-bought or homemade

*t*his delicious curry dish is great served over hot brown rice.

1 Place the shrimp in a large bowl and season with the salt and seafood seasoning; allow to marinate for 10 minutes.

2 Meanwhile, heat the olive oil in a large skillet over medium heat. Add the shallots, green and red peppers, and garlic and cook, stirring often, until the peppers are tender, about 6 minutes. Add the curry powder and cook for 1 minute. Add the shrimp and cook for 2 minutes.

3 Reduce the heat to low and stir in the chicken broth, 1 tablespoon of cream of coconut, and chili oil; simmer until the shrimp are completely done, about 8 minutes. (Refrigerate remaining cream of coconut in an airtight container for up to 5 days.) Serve immediately.

Makes 4 servings

TAKE NOTE

To make chili oil, combine 2 cups vegetable oil with 4 teaspoons crushed red pepper flakes in a small saucepan. Cook over low heat for 5 minutes. Remove from heat and allow to cool completely before transferring to a jar with an airtight lid. Store in the refrigerator for up to 1 month. Makes 2 cups.

Jerk Chicken Salad with Orange-Honey Vinaigrette

1 Place the chicken breasts in a resealable plastic bag and spoon the jerk marinade over the chicken. Seal and turn the chicken over to coat; refrigerate for 1 hour.

2 Spray a grill pan with nonstick cooking spray and heat over medium-high heat. Remove the chicken from the bag, discarding any remaining marinade. Grill the chicken about 5 minutes per side, or until cooked through. Remove chicken from the grill and place on a plate until cool enough to handle.

3 Meanwhile, in a jar with a tight-fitting lid, combine the vinegar, honey, olive oil, orange juice, and salt. Shake vigorously until well blended.

4 Place the chicken on a cutting board and slice into 1-inch slices.

5 To serve, place the spinach leaves in a large salad bowl and toss with 3 tablespoons of vinaigrette. Top with chicken, orange sections, and onions and drizzle with additional vinaigrette.

Makes 4 servings

4 boneless, skinless chicken breast halves

2 tablespoons jerk marinade (recommended: Walkerswood)

2 tablespoons cider vinegar

2 tablespoons honey

1 tablespoon extra virgin olive oil

2 tablespoons orange juice

Pinch of salt

One 10-ounce bag fresh spinach leaves, washed and dried thoroughly

2 large oranges, peeled and sectioned

1 small red onion, thinly sliced

Guess Who's Coming to Dinner?

"I Was Just in the Neighborhood" Menu

Smothered Turkey Wings

Big Ole Pot of Spaghetti with Meat Sauce

Chicken and Dumplings

Smothered Oxtails with Butter Beans

Simply Delicious Meatloaf

Old-Fashioned Double-Crust Peach Cobbler

i noticed when I started cooking that my friends would just drop by. Either they were "just in the area" or "hadn't heard from me in a minute and wanted to make sure I was okay." Whatever the excuse, the end result was always the same, "So, what are you cooking?" I would feel bad when I didn't have enough to go around (I've mastered cooking for two). So on occasion, I would make dishes that could feed an army, just in case. Usually, that was the day nobody would ring my bell and we'd be left with baked spaghetti casserole for the week . . . oh, well! The dishes in this section are perfect for those "just in the area" moments. —*Jeniece*

Smothered Turkey Wings

*S*erve these over white rice.

1 Preheat the oven to 350°F.

2 Rinse the turkey wings under cold water and pat dry with paper towels. Place the wings in a 9 by 13-inch baking dish and brush with the olive oil. In a small bowl, combine the Essential Seasoning, pepper, garlic powder, poultry seasoning, and onion powder. Sprinkle the wings with the spice mixture. Bake until browned, about 45 minutes.

3 Meanwhile, to make the gravy, melt the butter in a large skillet over medium heat; add the flour and cook, stirring, until light brown, about 5 minutes. Using a whisk, slowly stir in the warm water until combined. Season with the onion powder, Essential Seasoning, and thyme. Reduce the heat to low and simmer for 10 minutes after the gravy comes to a boil.

4 Remove the turkey wings from the oven and carefully pour the gravy over them. Cover with aluminum foil and place back into the oven until the turkey wings are tender, 45 to 60 minutes. Serve immediately.

Makes 4 to 6 servings

WINGS

2 pounds turkey wings, separated at the joints

¼ cup extra virgin olive oil

1 tablespoon Get 'Em Girl Essential Seasoning (page 16)

1 teaspoon ground black pepper

1 teaspoon garlic powder

1 teaspoon poultry seasoning

½ teaspoon onion powder

GRAVY

4 tablespoons (½ stick) unsalted butter

¼ cup all-purpose flour

3 cups warm water

¼ teaspoon onion powder

½ teaspoon Get 'Em Girl Essential Seasoning (page 16)

¼ teaspoon dried thyme

Big Ole Pot of Spaghetti with Meat Sauce

1 small onion, chopped

2 carrots, chopped

1 stalk celery, chopped

1 small red bell pepper, chopped

2 cloves garlic, minced

¼ cup extra virgin olive oil

2 pounds lean ground turkey

Salt and ground black pepper

1½ cups chicken broth

One 28-ounce can whole tomatoes, hand-crushed, with their juice

One 15-ounce can or two 8-ounce cans tomato sauce

½ teaspoon dried thyme

½ teaspoon dried oregano

2 fresh basil leaves

One 16-ounce package spaghetti

½ cup freshly grated Parmesan cheese

*t*his dish has saved us plenty of days when we were just building the company. We'd take turns making it and eat all week.

1 Place the onions, carrots, celery, bell pepper, and garlic in a food processor. Pulse the vegetables until finely chopped. Heat the olive oil in a Dutch oven over medium heat. Add the vegetables and cook, stirring often, until the vegetables are tender but not brown, about 7 minutes. Add the ground turkey and season with 1 teaspoon salt and ½ teaspoon pepper. Cook, breaking up the meat with the back of a wooden spoon, just until the meat is no longer pink, about 8 minutes.

2 Add the chicken broth to the meat mixture and cook, stirring frequently, until the liquid has reduced by half, about 10 minutes. Stir in the tomatoes with their juice and the tomato sauce. Season with ½ teaspoon salt, ½ teaspoon pepper, the thyme, and oregano. Add the basil. Bring to a boil, then reduce the heat to low and simmer, stirring occasionally, until the sauce is thick, 1 to 1½ hours. Remove from the heat, taste, and season with additional salt and pepper as necessary.

3 Meanwhile, bring a large pot of water to a boil. Season with salt and add the spaghetti. Cook according to the package directions until just tender. Drain in a colander and transfer to a serving bowl. Pour the meat sauce over the spaghetti and toss to coat; serve with Parmesan cheese.

Makes 4 to 6 servings

Chicken and Dumplings

*W*e went up to our local radio station one morning during our promo tour for the first book and my mother called in (how she continually gets through is beyond me — I guess she's just lucky like that). Anyway, she went on to talk about how one of the first things my dad asked her when they began dating was "Do you know how to make chicken and dumplings from scratch?" and she proudly said *"Hell, yes!"* Needless to say, my mommy is one of the original Get 'Em Girls! — *Jeniece*

1 Place the chicken, onions, celery, garlic, bay leaves, and bouillon cubes in a large saucepan. Season with the salt and pepper. Fill with enough water to cover the chicken. Bring to a simmer over medium heat. Cook until the chicken is tender and the juices run clear when pierced with a fork, about 35 minutes. Remove the bay leaves. Remove the chicken from the pot and, when it is cool enough to handle, remove the skin and separate the meat from the bones. Return the chicken meat to the pot and reduce heat to low.

2 Meanwhile, to make the dumplings: mix the flour and salt together in a large bowl and begin to slowly add the water to the flour, ¼ cup at a time. Mix with your hands after each addition to feel the consistency of the dough. Continue to add the water until the dough has come together and is slightly sticky. Turn the dough out onto a clean, floured work surface and turn the dough over onto itself to form into a ball. Roll out the dough with a rolling pin to ⅛-inch thickness. Using a sharp knife, cut into 1½-inch strips lengthwise.

3 Combine the cornstarch and water into a paste. Stir the cream, butter, and cornstarch mixture into the pot and raise the heat to medium. Bring to a boil and gently drop the dumplings, one at a time, into the boiling liquid. Push the dumplings down with a long-handled spoon, but do not stir. Cook until the dumplings are cooked through (no longer doughy in the center; the middle is firm), about 9 minutes, and remove from heat. To serve, ladle the chicken and dumplings into bowls.

Makes 6 servings

CHICKEN

One 2-pound chicken, cut up into 8 pieces

1 large onion, chopped

2 stalks celery, chopped

1 clove garlic, minced

2 bay leaves

2 chicken bouillon cubes

¼ teaspoon salt

½ teaspoon ground black pepper

2 tablespoons cornstarch

¼ cup water

½ cup heavy cream

2 tablespoons unsalted butter

DUMPLINGS

2 cups self-rising flour

1 teaspoon salt

¾ cup ice-cold water

Smothered Oxtails with Butter Beans

2 pounds oxtails, cut into 1-inch slices (have your butcher do this)

1½ teaspoons kosher salt

½ teaspoon ground black pepper

½ teaspoon garlic powder

½ cup all-purpose flour

2 tablespoons vegetable oil

2 cups low-sodium beef broth

2 cups chopped carrots

1 large onion, sliced into half-rings

2 bay leaves

½ teaspoon browning broth (optional)

One 16-ounce can butter beans, drained

1 Rinse and pat the oxtails dry. Season with the salt, pepper, and garlic powder. Dust the oxtails with the flour. Heat the vegetable oil in a Dutch oven over medium-high heat and add the oxtails to the pot. Brown the oxtails on all sides, then remove and set aside.

2 Add the beef broth to the pot and scrape up any browned bits at the bottom of the pot. Add the carrots, onions, bay leaves, and browning, if using, and stir in the oxtails. Reduce the heat to low, cover, and simmer, stirring occasionally, until the oxtails are tender, about 2 hours. Add the butter beans to the pot and cook for an additional 15 minutes; remove the bay leaves before serving.

Makes 4 to 6 servings

Simply Delicious Meatloaf

1 Preheat the oven to 375°F.

2 Heat the olive oil in a medium skillet over medium-high heat. Add the onions and cook just until tender, about 3 minutes. Add the mushrooms and season with salt. Cook, stirring occasionally, for 10 minutes. Add the garlic and cook for 5 minutes more. Remove from the heat and allow to cool completely.

3 Place the ground beef in a large bowl. Add the cooled mushrooms and mix well. In a separate bowl, mix together the bread crumbs, egg, ¼ cup of the tomato sauce, ¼ cup of the ketchup, the seasoned salt, pepper, and the onion and garlic powders. Mix into the ground beef and press in a 9 x 5 x 3-inch loaf pan.

4 In a small bowl, mix together the remaining tomato sauce and ketchup; spread on the top of the meatloaf. Cover with aluminum foil and bake for 45 minutes.

5 Remove the aluminum foil and place back in the oven to bake for 15 minutes more. Serve hot.

Makes 4 to 6 servings

2 tablespoons extra virgin olive oil

1 medium onion, chopped

1 cup sliced cremini mushrooms

½ cup sliced shiitake mushrooms

½ cup oyster mushrooms, trimmed

¼ teaspoon salt

1 clove garlic, minced

1½ pounds ground beef

½ cup fresh bread crumbs

1 large egg

½ cup tomato sauce

½ cup ketchup

1 teaspoon seasoned salt

½ teaspoon ground black pepper

¼ teaspoon onion powder

¼ teaspoon garlic powder

Old-Fashioned Double-Crust Peach Cobbler

Flaky Double Pie Crust
(recipe follows)

2 pounds frozen peaches, thawed

1½ teaspoons cornstarch

1 cup plus 1 tablespoon sugar

1 teaspoon fresh lemon juice

½ teaspoon ground cinnamon

1 teaspoon vanilla extract

4 tablespoons (½ stick) butter, chilled and cut into small pieces

1 large egg

1 teaspoon water

1 Preheat the oven to 350°F. Spray a 9 by 13-inch baking dish with nonstick cooking spray.

2 Cut the pie crust dough into two equal pieces. Place one-half in the refrigerator to keep cold. On a lightly floured surface, roll out half of the dough to a large rectangle ⅛ inch thick and big enough to fit the bottom of your baking dish. Prick it all over with a fork. Bake just until golden brown, about 5 minutes.

3 In a medium bowl, toss the peaches, cornstarch, 1 cup of the sugar, the lemon juice, cinnamon, and vanilla. Fold in the butter. Pour the peach mixture over the baked crust.

4 Roll out the second half of the pie crust on a lightly floured surface to a rectangle ⅛ inch thick and slightly larger than your baking dish. Cover the top of the baking dish with the dough and press down the edges of the dough with a fork onto the baking dish to seal. Using a small knife, cut slits in the top of the cobbler to vent. In a small bowl, mix the egg and water. Brush the top of cobbler with the egg wash. Sprinkle the remaining 1 tablespoon of sugar over the top of the cobbler. Bake until the crust is golden, 30 to 35 minutes. Serve warm or at room temperature.

Makes 8 servings

2 cups all-purpose flour

¾ teaspoon salt

⅔ cup vegetable shortening, chilled

½ cup ice-cold water

Flaky Double Pie Crust

In a medium bowl, sift together the flour and salt. Using a fork, cut the shortening into the flour until the mixture resembles small peas. Stirring with the fork, gradually add just enough of the water to make the mixture clump together. Gather up the dough and press into a thick disk. Divide into two disks and cover with plastic wrap. Refrigerate until ready to use.

Makes two 9-inch crusts

Meet the Friends
Dinner Party

"Let's All Be Friends" Menu
Feta and Spinach–Stuffed Chicken Breasts
Pesto Mashed Potatoes
All Day Lasagna
Banana-Walnut Monkey Bread

We've said it before, your grandmother told you, and we are saying it again: The way to a man's heart is through his stomach! Well, we want to add to that . . . The way to a man's heart is through his *and* his friends' stomachs!

Feta and Spinach–Stuffed Chicken Breasts

Serve these with your favorite pasta.

1 Preheat the oven to 350°F. Mix the feta, broccoli, spinach, tomato, and onion and garlic powders in a small bowl.

2 Cover each chicken breast in plastic wrap and flatten with a rolling pin to ½ inch thickness.

3 Divide the stuffing into four portions and place a portion in the center of each chicken breast. Wrap breasts around the stuffing tightly, securing chicken with toothpicks.

4 Place the chicken on a baking sheet seam side down. Sprinkle the mozzarella on top.

5 Bake for 40 to 45 minutes or until the chicken is golden brown and fully cooked (edges might be slightly crispy).

Makes 4 servings

½ cup crumbled feta cheese

½ cup frozen broccoli florets, thawed and chopped

½ cup frozen spinach, thawed and drained

1 medium tomato, diced

1 teaspoon onion powder

1 teaspoon garlic powder

4 whole boneless, skinless, chicken breasts, halved

¼ cup shredded low-fat mozzarella cheese

Pesto Mashed Potatoes

2½ pounds Russet potatoes, peeled and cut into 1-inch chunks

Salt

4 tablespoons (½ stick) unsalted butter, plus extra for serving

¼ cup half-and-half

Ground black pepper

3 tablespoons jarred pesto

1 Place the potatoes in a large pot with ½ teaspoon salt and add water to cover. Bring to a boil over high heat. Reduce the heat to a simmer, cover, and cook until the potatoes are fork tender, 15 to 20 minutes. Using a colander, drain the potatoes. Place them back into the pot. Add the butter and mash with a potato masher until smooth.

2 In a small saucepan, heat the half-and-half over low heat until warm. Stir the half-and-half into the mashed potatoes and mix just until combined. Season with salt and pepper to taste. Stir in the pesto and transfer to a serving dish. Serve immediately with additional butter.

Makes 4 servings

All Day Lasagna

1 Preheat the oven to 375°F. Bring a large pot of salted water to a boil over medium-high heat.

2 To make the sauce, heat 3 tablespoons of the olive oil in a heavy-bottomed large pot over medium heat. Add the onions and cook, stirring occasionally, until softened, about 5 minutes. Season lightly with a pinch of salt and pepper, add the garlic to the pot, and continue to cook until fragrant, about 1 minute.

3 Add the beef bones to the pot and cook, turning, until the meat is browned on all sides. Add the ground beef and pork to the pot and season with 1 tablespoon of salt and 1½ teaspoons of ground pepper; cook, breaking up the meat with a wooden spoon, until the meat has fully browned and the fat has begun to evaporate, about 15 minutes.

4 Pour in the chicken broth and stir in the bay leaf, oregano, and thyme. Bring to a boil and cook, scraping up the brown bits at the bottom of the pot, until the chicken broth is almost completely evaporated. Pour in the tomatoes, then stir in the tomato paste until it is dissolved. Add the sugar and season with 1 teaspoon of salt. Reduce the heat to low and cook, uncovered, stirring occasionally and skimming off any fat that has risen to the top, until the sauce begins to thicken slightly and deepen in color, about 45 minutes to 1 hour. Discard the beef marrow bones when the sauce has fully cooked.

5 Meanwhile, bring another large pot of salted water and 2 tablespoons of olive oil to a boil. Line a baking sheet with parchment paper and set aside.

6 When the water begins to boil, stir in one-third of the lasagna noodles and cook until just tender, about 8 to 10 minutes. Using a set of pincer tongs, take the noodles out of the water and lay in one layer on the parchment-lined baking sheet. Place another layer of parchment paper over the cooked noodles and repeat the cooking and stacking process with the remaining two batches of noodles.

7 While the noodles are cooking, stir the ricotta, eggs, and 1 cup of the Parmesan cheese together in a medium bowl and season lightly with salt and pepper until well blended.

5 tablespoons extra virgin olive oil

1 small onion, chopped

Salt and ground black pepper

2 cloves garlic, peeled

1 pound beef marrow bones

1½ pounds ground beef

1½ pounds ground pork

1 cup low-sodium chicken or beef broth

1 bay leaf

1¼ teaspoons dried oregano

½ teaspoon dried thyme

Two 28-ounce cans whole tomatoes, hand-crushed, with their juice

2 tablespoons tomato paste

1 tablespoon sugar

Two 16-ounce packages lasagna noodles

One 15-ounce container ricotta cheese, drained

2 large eggs

2 cups freshly grated Parmesan cheese

One 16-ounce package mozzarella cheese, sliced

8 To assemble the lasagna, spoon 1 cup of the meat sauce over the bottom of an extra deep 10 x 15-inch baking dish. Arrange noodles lengthwise, overlapping the noodles if necessary, to cover the bottom of the baking dish. Spoon about 2 cups of meat sauce over the noodles, to cover completely, and sprinkle with ½ cup of Parmesan cheese. Arrange another layer of noodles lengthwise and spread the ricotta cheese mixture over the noodles. Arrange a third layer of noodles over the ricotta and place the mozzarella slices over the noodles in a single layer.

9 Spoon about 1 cup of meat sauce over the layer of mozzarella and cover with another layer of noodles. Spoon the remaining meat sauce over the noodles and spread to cover the noodles completely. Sprinkle with the remaining ½ cup of Parmesan cheese and cover loosely with aluminum foil. Bake for 40 minutes and remove the aluminum foil. Continue to bake for an additional 15 to 20 minutes and remove from the oven. Allow to cool for 15 minutes before cutting into squares and serving.

Makes about 18 servings

Banana-Walnut Monkey Bread

1 Preheat the oven to 350°F. Spray a 12-cup fluted pan with nonstick cooking spray.

2 Mix the granulated sugar and cinnamon together in a medium bowl and set aside. Begin pulling apart 2-inch pieces of Monkey Bread dough, dredging them in the cinnamon-sugar mixture, and setting aside on a clean work surface. Slice the bananas into ½-inch slices and set aside. Flatten each piece of cinnamon-sugar-covered dough in the palm of your hand and place a banana slice in the middle of each piece. Cover the banana completely with dough by pulling the sides of the dough over the banana and pinching to tighten; continue with remaining banana slices and dough.

3 In a small saucepan over low heat, melt the butter and brown sugar together and stir until the brown sugar has completely melted, then stir in the walnuts.

4 Layer half of the prepared dough in the bottom of the tube pan and spoon half of the brown sugar–walnut mixture over the top. Repeat with the remaining dough and brown sugar–walnut mixture.

5 Bake for 18 to 20 minutes and remove from the oven. Let stand for 3 minutes. Place a plate on top of the tube pan and invert the monkey bread. Serve warm.

Makes 8 to 10 servings

½ cup granulated sugar

2 teaspoons cinnamon

One recipe for Monkey Bread Dough (page 192)

4 large ripe bananas

8 tablespoons (1 stick) unsalted butter

½ cup dark brown sugar, packed tightly

1½ cups chopped walnuts

1 package active dry yeast

¼ teaspoon sugar

¼ cup warm water (110–115°F)

¼ cup warm milk (110–115°F)

¼ cup sugar

1 teaspoon salt

2 tablespoons unsalted butter

2 tablespoons vegetable shortening

2 large eggs

2½ cups all-purpose flour, plus
more for dusting

Monkey Bread Dough

1 In a small bowl, dissolve yeast and ¼ teaspoon sugar in warm water; let stand 5 minutes. In a separate bowl, with an electric mixer, beat together the milk, ¼ cup sugar, salt, butter, shortening, and eggs. Add the yeast mixture and beat thoroughly. Add the flour to the yeast mixture and mix just until the dough comes together.

2 Turn dough out onto a well-floured surface; knead until dough is smooth and elastic, about 5 minutes, then shape dough into a ball. Spray a large bowl with nonstick cooking spray; place dough in prepared bowl, turn dough over once, and cover with a kitchen towel. Let the dough rise in a warm place until it doubles in size, about 1½ to 2 hours.

Cocktail Time!

Let Me Call You a Cab

Get 'Em Girl Pom Punch

Cocoa Cure Chocolate Martini

Goshay Cocktail

Key Lime Pie Martini

Cheryl's Deluxe Frozen Margaritas

Poppin' Black Cherry Martini

Cranberry Daiquiri

Aunt Melody's Bloody Mary

Virgins Only

Cranberry Punch

Shakara's Virgin Piña Colada

Get 'Em Girl Shimosa

*C*ongratulations! You've made it through another long week...TGEGIF (Thank Get 'Em Girls It's Friday). Your girlfriends are on the way over and you've got the food in order. Now it's time to make sure your drinks are on point. Wait, scratch that. You and your girls want to get your drink on and you want to do it in a safe environment, so when Nikki turns into La Niña, you don't have to figure out how to get her drunken butt home. Enjoy these alcoholic and nonalcoholic drinks and don't forget to select a designated driver, have plenty of cab numbers on hand, or plenty of blankets for an impromptu slumber party!

So you've got your two-step ready—all you need now is a great drink. Below are the essentials needed to stock your bar.

Liquors

Brandy or Cognac
Bourbon
Gin
Irish Cream
Rum (light and dark)
Scotch
Vodka
Tequila
Whiskey
Beer

Liqueurs

Fruit-flavored liqueurs (orange, cherry, peach, raspberry, apple, and melon)
Amaretto
Coffee liqueurs (Kahlúa)
Chocolate liqueurs

Mixers

Cola

Ginger Ale

Lemon-lime soda

Club soda

Sour mix

Bitters

Grenadine

Fruit Juices and Nectars

Cranberry

Pomegranate

Lemon

Lime

Orange

Pineapple

Tomato

Apple

Peach

Passion fruit

Get 'Em Girl Pom Punch

4 cups pomegranate juice
(recommended: POM)

2 cups orange juice

One 12-ounce can frozen limeade
concentrate, thawed

One 750-ml bottle sparkling wine

Ice cubes

Lime slices, for garnish

We are city girls with Southern roots and we usually find ourselves on a hot summer day sipping on this cold cocktail on the terrace watching the pigeons walk by. Enjoy this delicious sparkling punch wherever you are with great company.

Stir together the pomegranate juice, orange juice, and limeade in a martini pitcher. Slowly pour in the sparkling wine. Serve over ice in a cocktail glass garnished with lime slices.

Makes 10 servings

Cocoa Cure Chocolate Martini

*t*his decadent martini smells just as good as it tastes!

Wet the rims of four martini glasses with a little water and dip into the cocoa powder; set aside. Pour the vodka and crème de cacao into a cocktail shaker filled with ice and shake vigorously. Strain into the prepared martini glasses and serve immediately.

Makes 4 servings

Cocoa powder for rims of glasses, unsweetened

1 cup vanilla-flavored vodka

¼ cup crème de cacao, dark

Ice cubes

Goshay Cocktail

½ cup cognac (recommended:
Hennessy)

1½ cups apple juice

Ice cubes

*O*ur hair stylist Tamika is the business when it comes to a
fierce haircut *and* a lethal cocktail! In fact, anytime we enter
the "shop" and see the blender out on a Friday evening, we know
we are in for a long night at Trax! This cocktail is an adaptation
of her favorite concoction of green apple coolers topped off with
a shot of Hennessy.

Pour the cognac and apple juice into a cocktail shaker filled with ice and
shake. Strain into cocktail glasses filled with ice.

Makes 4 servings

Key Lime Pie Martini

i tried this drink at a hotel in Charlotte and I was so surprised by how good it was. Needless to say, it's a favorite now!

—Joan

Combine the vodka, pineapple juice, melon liqueur, coconut rum, lime juice, soda, and half-and-half in a cocktail shaker half-filled with ice. Shake well and strain into a chilled cocktail glass garnished with the lime slice. Serve.

Makes 1 serving

¼ cup vanilla-flavored vodka

2 tablespoons pineapple juice

2 tablespoons melon liqueur (recommended: Midori)

2 tablespoons coconut-flavored rum

1 tablespoon Rose's lime juice

Splash of lemon-lime soda

Splash of half-and-half

Ice cubes

Lime slice, for garnish

Cheryl's Deluxe Frozen Margaritas

Ice cubes

One 10-ounce can frozen Margarita drink mix (recommended: Bacardi)

½ cup plus 2 tablespoons tequila (recommended: Patrón Silver)

½ cup plus 2 tablespoons triple sec

6 tablespoons sugar

2 tablespoons orange liqueur (recommended: Grand Marnier)

We first had these at Russ and Cheryl's house on New Year's Eve and we knew right away that she was going to have to give up the recipe. Sip slowly and enjoy!

1 Fill a blender with ice and add the drink mix, tequila, triple sec, and 4 tablespoons of the sugar. Blend until smooth and frothy. Place in the freezer until ready to serve.

2 When ready to serve, dip the rim of each glass into the orange liqueur and then into the remaining sugar; pour the margarita evenly into standard-size margarita glasses and serve immediately.

Makes 4 servings

Poppin' Black Cherry Martini

i tasted a drink very similar to this while in Charlotte and I was hooked! The candy rim is just an added little kick to an already delicious cocktail. —*Jeniece*

1 Pour the Pop Rocks out into a small shallow dish. Wet the rim of a cocktail glass with a little water and dip into the Pop Rocks; set aside.

2 Combine the vodka, schnapps, soda, cranberry juice, and grenadine in a cocktail shaker half-filled with ice. Shake well and strain into the prepared cocktail glass. Garnish with the cherry and serve.

Makes 1 serving

1 packet Pop Rocks candy

¼ cup black cherry vodka

2 tablespoons cherry schnapps

2 tablespoons lemon-lime soda

1 tablespoon cranberry juice cocktail

1 tablespoon grenadine

Ice cubes

Maraschino cherry, for garnish

Cranberry Daiquiri

2 cups cranberry juice cocktail

½ cup fresh lemon juice
(about 5 lemons)

½ cup fresh lime juice
(about 6 limes)

½ cup sugar

⅓ cup light rum

Ice cubes

Fresh cranberries, for garnish

Mix together the cranberry juice, lemon and lime juices, sugar, and rum in a large pitcher until the sugar is completely dissolved. Pour into a blender and fill with ice. Blend on the ice-crush setting until the mixture is slushy. Pour into 8-ounce daiquiri glasses and garnish with fresh cranberries.

Makes 4 servings

Aunt Melody's Bloody Mary

*W*hen my family gets together you can count on three things: a Spades game that just won't quit, Uncle Larry's Fried Whiting (page 79), and Aunt Melody's Bloody Mary, which is usually reserved for the elders—even I'm not grown up enough to partake! — *Jeniece*

Pour the vodka, tomato juice, celery salt, Worcestershire, and hot pepper sauce in a cocktail shaker filled with ice. Season to taste with salt and pepper and shake vigorously until combined. Strain into hurricane glasses filled with ice and garnish with a celery stalk with a pepper ring around it.

Makes 2 servings

½ cup plus 2 tablespoons vodka

1¼ cups tomato juice

¼ teaspoon celery salt

¼ teaspoon Worcestershire sauce

2 dashes of hot pepper sauce

Ice cubes

Salt and ground black pepper to taste

Celery stalks, for garnish

Green bell pepper rings, for garnish

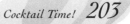

Cranberry Punch

4 cups cranberry juice cocktail

1½ cups sugar or Splenda

4 cups pineapple juice

2 liters ginger ale

Ice cubes

a delicious and refreshing punch that is perfect for a get-together over brunch with family and friends.

Combine the cranberry juice, sugar, and pineapple juice. Mix until the sugar dissolves. Refrigerate. Just before serving, add the ginger ale. Serve over ice.

Makes 4 quarts

Shakara's Virgin Piña Colada

*M*y favorite non-alcoholic beverage. I just have to be sure to pour a glass as soon as I make it because Jeniece and Joan are just waiting to spike the leftover mix. — *Shakara*

Fill a blender with ice and add the coconut cream and pineapple juice. Blend until smooth and frosty. Pour the drink into two glasses. Garnish with the pineapple slices and cherries.

Makes 2 servings

Ice cubes

2 cans coconut creme (recommended: Coco Lopez)

2 cups pineapple juice

Pineapple slices, for garnish

Cherries, for garnish

Get 'Em Girl Shimosa

¼ cup orange juice

¾ cup lemon-lime soda

2 tablespoons grenadine

*t*his is a fusion of the famous Shirley Temple and the brunch favorite, mimosa. Enjoy this alcohol-free cocktail with adults and teens alike.

Pour the orange juice into a tall glass and fill with lemon-lime soda. Gently stir in the grenadine and serve.

Makes 1 serving

Kitchen 101

Dry Measure Conversion

Cup	Fluid Ounce	Tablespoon	Teaspoon	Milliliter
1	8	16	48	237
¾	6	12	36	177
⅔	5⅓	10⅔	32	158
½	4	8	24	118
⅓	2⅔	5⅓	16	79
¼	2	4	12	59
⅛	1	2	6	30

Liquid Measure Conversion

Cup	Pint	Quart	Fluid Ounce	Liter
16	8	4	128	3.79
8	4	2	64	1.89
4	2	1	32	0.95
2	1	½	16	0.47
1	½	¼	8	0.24
½			4	0.12
¼			2	0.06
⅛			1	0.03

Oven Temperature Conversion

°F	°C
200	95
250	120
275–300	135–150
300–325	150–165
325–350	165–180
350–375	180–190
375–400	190–205
400–425	205–220
425–450	220–230
450–475	230–245
475–500	245–260

Index

walnut(s):

   -banana monkey bread, 191

   candied, in spinach and roasted pear salad with pomegranate vinaigrette, 173

warm vanilla tea cakes, 104

white bean dip with pita crisps, 68

white chocolate ganache, chocolate bread pudding with, 50

whiting, Uncle Larry's fried, 79

whole cranberry relish, 148

wine, 11–12

   serving temperatures for, 12

wings:

   Danni's honey barbecue, 66

   smothered turkey, 179

wontons, chocolate kiss, 138

wood chips, grilling with, 94

Y

yogurt:

   parfait, honey banana crunch, 120

   in rise-and-shine breakfast smoothies, 51